RAGHU PALAT is an acknowledged authority on investment, finance and banking and has written more than thirty extremely well received books on these subjects.

A great grandson of His Highness, the late Rama Varma, Maharaja of Cochin, and Sir Chettur Sankaran Nair, a member of the Viceroy's Privy Council and a former President of the Indian National Congress, Raghu Palat is a Fellow of the Institute of Chartered Accountants in England & Wales.

A career banker he has held very senior positions with multinational banks in India and abroad. He has worked in Europe, America, Asia and Africa.

Raghu Palat is presently a banking consultant. He also manages a dedicated finance portal www.banking-rules.com which is a repertoire of rules and regulations relating to finance, commerce, corporates and banks. In addition, he conducts workshops on business etiquette, effective business writing, presentation skills, banking and finance.

Mr. Palat has also set up a portal for e-learning www.ibbc.co.in. The courses are an amalgam of laws, directives and actual real life situations.

Raghu Palat lives in Mumbai with his wife Pushpa.

Also by Raghu Palat

~

Fiction

Anguish

~

Non Fiction

Tax Planning for the Salaried Employees

~

The Credit Report

~

The Wonderworld of Investments

~

How to Read Annual Reports and Balance Sheets

~

Investments – Where and When

~

Understanding Financial Ratios in Business

~

Fundamental Analysis for Investors

~

Documentary Letters of Credit and Collections

~

How to Apply for a Bank Loan and Get it Sanctioned

~

How to Manage Foreign Exchange Risks

~

Effective Business Writing

~

A Complete Guide for the NRI

~

Everything Indians Need to Know on Business Etiquette

~

Interview Tips – Get the Job You Want

~

Secrets of their Success – Achievers from the World of Finance

~

Corporate Leaders – Secrets of their Success

~

Retail Banking – Everything you need to know to work in a bank

~

Self Made High Achievers – Secrets of their Success

~

The Bank of India Story – Relationships Beyond Banking

~

Basic Banking

~

Banking Fundamentals

~

The Negotiable Instruments Act

~

Retail Banking

Shares for Investment and Wealth

3rd Edition

A Guide to Investing Wisely in the Stock Market

Raghu Palat

www.visionbooksindia.com

www.visionbooksindia.com

Disclaimer

The opinions expressed in this book are those of the author and those he has spoken to and must not be construed as the opinion of any other person, company or institution.

This book is sold with the clear understanding that the author, the publisher, the distributor, the resellers and anyone else involved with this book are not responsible for or liable for the result of an action taken (based on a suggestion made or opinion expressed in this book) by the reader or for any other error or omission.

First Published 1991
Second Edition, 2007
Third Edition, 2016
Reprinted, 2025

ISBN 10: 81-7094-971-8
ISBN 13: 978-81-7094-971-8

Published by
Vision Books Pvt. Ltd.
(Incorporating Orient Paperbacks and CARING imprints)
24 Feroze Gandhi Road, Lajpat Nagar 3
New Delhi 110024, India.
Phone: (+91-11) 2984 0821 / 22
e-mail: visionbooks@gmail.com

Printed at
Saurabh Printers
67A-68, Ecotech 1, Extn 1, Kasna, Greater Noida
Uttar Pradesh, India.

Audentis Fortuna Juvat

(Fortune favours the bold)

— *Virgil*

Contents

Preface

When it was originally published in 1991, this book was among the first books to focus on the Indian stock market. The book's intent was to unravel the mysteries and hidden secrets of the stock market for the individual investor and make him or her aware of its huge potential. I believe it fulfilled this admirably and was appreciated. It was for several months on the best seller list of many newspapers.

Mr. M. R. Mayya, former Executive Director of the Bombay Stock Exchange stated in his 1991 foreword to this book:

> Raghu Palat introduces the reader to investment in shares by explaining the various basic concepts of investment in shares. The book is lucid in style, easy to understand and introduces the reader systematically to the various strategies and risks involved. As President Franklin D. Roosevelt of the United States of America observed while signing the Securities Act of 1933, the object should be to change the concept from *caveat emptor* (buyer beware) to caveat vendor (seller beware). The collective efforts of all of us should be to ensure that we in India translate this object into reality. Raghu Palat's book is an effort in this direction as it will educate the readers on the skills required for successful investment in stock markets.

The stock market continues to excite the investing public. The potential of huge gains and mind-shattering profits continues to lure people. I do not believe this popular attraction to the market will ever die.

This is why I decided to revise the earlier editions. Revision is necessary as there have been mind-blowing changes in the last twenty five years — The National Stock Exchange (NSE) was conceived and established; market regulator Securities and Exchange Board of India (SEBI) has been established and is made its presence felt; shares have been dematerialised; new issues are being book built; Foreign Institutional Investors and Mutual Funds are now significant presences; the individual small investor's focus has changed. In addition, during this time, scams have rocked the markets during this period — the Harshad Mehta scam and the Ketan Parekh scam leading to greater transparency and tighter controls. In 2006 the initial public offer (IPO) scam and the "know your customer" (KYC) stipulations not being strictly adhered to resulted in SEBI seeking disgorgement fines from certain depository participants. The global financial meltdown of 2008 was significant — the Bombay Stock Exchange Sensitivity Index (Sensex) fell from 21,000 to below 9,000. The coming into power of the Bharatiya Janata Party (BJP) with Narendra Modi at the helm in 2014 saw the markets boom as "*acche din*" (good days) were anticipated. It stabilised and fell when the reforms anticipated did not materialise as expected. A phenomenon today is that India is no longer insular as it was twenty-five years ago. Global events such as the ISIS threat, the happenings in Syria, the Federal Funds Rate and such likes have a marked effect on the index. The Sensex which hovered around 2,000 in 1991 to 15,000 in 2006, to over 27,000 by 2016. Trading volumes in the equity segment have grewn rapidly with average daily turnover increasing from ₹ 17 crore during 1994-95 to ₹ 6,253 crore during 2005-06 to ₹ 43,621 crore in 2015 with 26,059 lakh transactions. Market capitalization rose from ₹ 3,00,000 crore in 1991 to over ₹ 3,500,000 crore in March 2007 and to ₹ 10,420,430 crore in December 2015. With more that 5,500 listed companies the Bombay Stock Exchange (BSC) is today the largest in the world in terms of listed members.

Even though the book has been updated I have kept many of the examples mentioned in the earlier edition as they still stand and are valid. The reader should therefore absorb the point being made, rather than worry about the data *per se*.

This book is the result of years of research and practical experience of years of trading and of reading everything I could lay my hands on that had anything to do with the stock market. The subject is fascinating. The research has been absorbing. The experience has been enriching.

During conversations with my friends, acquaintances and strangers, the fact that disturbed me most was that though these individuals were learned, wise and experts in their chosen fields, they were infants in the world of shares, and like infants they dabbled in the market without really knowing why they were buying or selling. They bought because their cousin whose cousin knew a broker said to buy — and sold for some similar reason! Some lost. Most made some money. But then they could have made much more, if they had paid more heed and determined a strategy.

I want to share my knowledge with you. Herodotus said over 2,500 years ago:

> There is nothing more profitable for a man than to take good counsel with himself; for even if the events turn out contrary to one's hope, still one's decision was right, even though fortune has made it of no effect; whereas if a man acts contrary to good counsel, although by luck he gets what he has no right to expect, his decision was not any the less foolish.

This book is for the individual investor — the professional, the housewife, the salaried employee, the executive, the student, the budding entrepreneur and anyone else who works hard and has some money to spare. It is for him or her who wants to unravel the mysteries of the world of stocks and shares and experience the excitement and thrills of trading with its risks and promise of stupendous gains. This book will introduce you to the world of shares — the kinds of shares there are, how they may be acquired and sold, the factors that should be considered prior to the purchase or sale of shares, the strategies that could be adopted, and the manner in which a portfolio should be managed. These will help you enter and stay in the arena. For those already there, this book will serve you as a guide, a reference book to remind you of how to continue in the market — to help you evolve new strategies and to win.

I'd also like to quote Charles Lamb, "You may derive thoughts from others. Your way of thinking, the mould in which your thoughts are cast must be your own."

I gratefully acknowledge the information and knowledge that I have received from reading business periodicals, papers, articles and books on stocks and the stock markets. These are too many to individually enumerate. They were all well researched, informative and absorbing.

I have profited and learnt from my discussions and talks with my friends in the press and in the financial world. I am aware of the hours of their time that they gave to me unstintingly and so willingly.

It was my father-in-law, the late Mr. K.V.A. Nair of Kolkata, who unwittingly introduced me to the delights of the stock markets. I cherish the talks I have had with him and miss his counsel. His knowledge was so vast; his perceptions were so clear. Every conversation was a learning experience.

I thank my wife Pushpa. She has been wonderful — encouraging, critical and patient. It was she who urged me to write. It was she who read my first attempts, criticized them, typed them and gave me the courage to publish. But for her, I would not have written a single article or book.

My daughters Divya and Nikhila must bear some responsibility for this book. Their pride and unconcealed delight in seeing my name in print fuels me on to write. What greater faith can one ask for?

And above all, I have enjoyed writing this book. I hope you do too.

Happy investing.

October 2016
Mumbai

RAGHU PALAT

Introduction

Ever since the world's first important stock exchange — a roofless courtyard in Amsterdam — began operations in 1611, this market more than any other has excited, ruined and made rich more men than any other institution. It has whetted the appetite and the gambling instincts of so many people that De La Vega's epithet of the Amsterdam Stock Exchange of the sixteen eighties was "this gambling hell." He went on to say, "It is foolish to think that you can withdraw from the exchange after you have tasted the sweetness of the honey." It is extremely addictive. This is why John Brooks in his book *Business Adventures* called the market, "the daytime adventure serial of the well to do."

The magic of the stock market burst upon the Indian investor during the late 1970s when the erstwhile foreign companies Indianized. Shares in these profitable companies were offered to an eager public and as prices rose and demand grew, the interest of the Indian public was whetted. This interest grew in the 1980s and early 1990s but suffered a set back in the wake of the Harshad Mehta scam which exploded in 1992. India's economic liberalization which began in July 1991 gave the market fresh impetus and after a lull during the South East Asian crises and the economic downturn at the turn of the millennium, the market was again vibrant and throbbing. After the Ketan Mehta scam in the early years of the new millennium, the market fell, but again revived in 2005. It rose shortly after that to fall in the meltdown of 2008. After the victory of the Bharatiya Janata Party and the euphoria that followed the Sensex soared to nearly 30,000.

For a variety of reasons, including turmoil in Europe the market Sensex fell by a little over 20%. However, companies in India are sound. India has the potential and if the economic growth happens as planned, India would to be among biggest and most profitable markets in the world.

What attracts one to the stock market? What makes it so fascinating — so fascinating that it was likened by Adam Smith in *The Money Game* to a beautiful woman — "endlessly fascinating, endlessly complex, always changing, always mystifying." It is the promise it holds of great wealth and the stories of those who have become millionaires. The tragedies of lives ruined, the great Wall Street crash and other financial catastrophes are discounted and forgotten in the wake of the possibility of monies to be made.

To my mind one of the greatest attractions is the opportunity to demonstrate that one can be ahead of the crowd. As soon as the Battle of Waterloo was won, Nathan Rothschild had arranged for carrier pigeons to be dispatched to him to inform him of the outcome. On receiving the news, Rothschild went into the market and began to sell his shares. This created a panic. Assuming that the battle was lost everyone began to sell and the bottom fell out of the market. Rothschild with his intermediaries bought and bought and by the time the official messenger with the dispatches arrived, Rothschild has made a fortune. Thus was born one of the great principles of successful investing, "buy when there is blood on the streets."

Is there anyone who has not heard of Polly Peck, the rag trade company into which the Turkish-Cypriot economics graduate Asil Nadir breathed the gift of life? Nadir bought the company and developed it into a fruit trading and electronics empire. In ten years Nadir's growth by acquisition strategy increased the company's market capitalization from only GBP 300,000 to GBP 731 million. The price of its shares soared from 9 pence to GBP 36. Anyone who invested GBP 2,500 before the takeover became a millionaire. This is the stuff legends are made of.

Or what of Haloid? Haloid was a small company attempting to, manufacture duplicating machines by xerography. The University of Rochester, partly out of interest in struggling local industry, bought for its endowment fund a large number of shares at a price which because of bonus issues or splits amounted to about fifty cents a share. They warned the chief executive of Haloid that they may be forced to sell the shares in a few years "to cut our losses." Haloid was successful. The machine was a success. The company was renamed Xerox and the University made a profit of $100 million. And to think that at one time, the chief executive of Haloid, Wilson and his colleagues were so fed up that they considered selling their xerography rights to IBM. Fortunately (for them) the deal was called off. Between 1947 and 1955, Wilson and the other executives of the company took most of their pay in the form of stock. Some bought shares by mortgaging their houses and encashed their savings to help the company. When the process became a success in 1960, instead of worrying about their future, Xerox executives worried about their reputation with friends and relatives — people whom they had prudently advised not to invest in the stock which was then selling at 20 cents a share. Anyone who had Xerox stock in reasonable quantity became rich — richer than they had ever dreamed possible.

Nearer home, when Infosys had its initial public offering in 1993 the offer was undersubscribed and a large portion devolved on the underwriters; Morgan Stanley was forced to pick up 13% of the shares. The apparent distress of the underwriters later became their delight when Infosys became the wealth creator that it is.

After the FERA dilution and just prior to liberalization in 1991, the market in India opened up. This was just before the Harshad Mehta scam horrified the investing public. Before the scam came to light, everyone but everyone bought shares, often at the flimsiest of excuses. I remember being surprised and delighted to hear at a party several lady home makers discussing not recipes and clothes but shares and industry trends. When the Harshad Mehta scam became public, thousands of investors, greedy to make unrealistic profits, lost hugely and the markets went into a tailspin. Then, following liberalization, the character of investors changed with the coming into India of foreign institutional investors and mutual funds. The individual investor is no longer the most important — the institutional investor is. The trust and the comfort of the Indian investor were further eroded by the Ketan Parekh scam in 2001, following which, the Indian individual investor laid low till 2004. In 2004, the share market began moving up again after years of being in the doldrums. Even the Reliance imbroglio did not dampen sentiments. In 2005, with prices of most shares rising and the economy growing, the market began once again to look up. There was a little concern in May 2006 when Sensex fell by over 800 points in one day and slid in a short time from 12,600 to under 8,000. However, it then recovered and crossed 14,000. It had nearly reached 15,000 but it dipped after the budget falling to nearly 12,500. It rose to nearly 21,000 and then with the global meltdown of 2008 fell to under 9,000. After that it recovered and got a huge boost with the parliamentary electoral victory of the Bharatiya Janata Party (BJP) under the leadership of Narendra Modi. The Sensex in a short time rose to nearly 30,000. However, with reforms not being implemented as quickly as hoped and the refugee crisis in Europe the Sensex again fell in November 2015 to just over 25,000. Where will the Sensex go next? It is difficult to say. One thing is certain, though. History will repeat itself and over time the rise in equities will be higher than that of any other investment.

Investing in the stock market is, in my opinion, the only avenue available to the common man to stay ahead of inflation.

In addition, the market has all the ingredients of an adventure — the risks, the elation, the hopes, the optimism and the tragedy. Playing the market is fun and I love it.

I want to share this fun and the excitement with you — from the initial choice of a share to invest into its actual purchase and the eventual sale. I want to worry with you while you hold the share — while it rises to an unanticipated high or falls to a disastrous low.

I learnt about the stock market the only way one can — by actually buying shares and losing money. I made mistakes. I did not know what to look for. I did not know investment strategies. I was a pig losing money in the markets where both bulls and bears were turning straw into gold. In time I learnt what to look out for.

This book is for you — the new investor, the student investor, the housewife investor and any other individual investor who has flirted with the market and is not as yet a professional. This book introduces you to the things that you should look for, matters you should consider, and suggests strategies that you could adopt. This book warns you of the pitfalls that you should avoid and alerts you to the errors that you might make.

There is a lot to learn. A lot is learnt by experience. A lot too is learnt by reading and listening to the advice given to you by others. This book attempts to be a bridge between the two.

Finally, you do not need a fortune to begin playing the market. You can begin with as little as ₹ 10,000. You do not need to understand the language or have a massive database residing in a computer at home or in the office. What you need in a nutshell is common sense, luck and commitment. If you have these, shares can make you a millionaire and even if you don't become one — trading in the market will give you many enjoyable hours of fun and excitement.

~

Chapter 1

~

The Principles of Investment

The purpose of investment is to make one's capital grow. The investor's predominant desire is to ensure that his capital will not erode and that his wealth will increase. Consequently, prior to making an investment, all serious investors will necessarily ask the following questions:

- Is the investment safe?
- Is the investment liquid?
- Will it yield income and, if so, how much?
- Will its value appreciate?

Safety of Investment

The first and possibly the most basic question that an investor seeks an answer to is whether the investment is safe. This question gains very great importance if the amount the investor intends to invest is a disproportionately large part of his capital. Should the investment turn out to be a failure, a lemon, then the investor could be ruined. A certain amount of risk exists with every investment. Investment return correlates inversely with safety. The greater the risk, the higher the return. This is why the return one earns on bank deposits is the lowest. The risk of the loss of capital is practically non-existent. On the other hand, the returns on loans made are among the highest.

This is due to the very real possibility that the loans may not be repaid.

Liquidity

Liquidity is the term used to describe the ease with which an investment can be turned into cash. This is very important as an investor may sometimes need to convert his investment into cash very fast. Real estate is an asset and it can never be converted in a big hurry. Even certain savings instruments are not very liquid. National Saving Certificates cannot be encashed for six years. Similarly, there is a lock-in period for several equity linked investment schemes. On the other hand, equity shares of companies listed on the stock exchange are extremely liquid and marketable. Shares of private companies not listed on any stock exchange can be, on the other hand, illiquid as no one may want them.

Income Yield

The investor's main criterion (and rightly so) in choosing an investment is often the income that he will earn on the investment. As noted earlier, the greater the risk, the higher the income or yield. And the opposite is true, too. This, therefore, is usually the deciding factor. Consequently, it is prudent to remember a few points.

Inflation

It is important that the return is as much as, if not greater than, the rate of inflation. Otherwise there will be a steady deterioration of capital. Especially so if one spends more than the income received. From this point of view, bank deposits though very safe, are the worst type of investments one can make. The maximum return that one will receive on a 3-year deposit is around 9% per annum. This will vary based on the Reserve Bank of India's credit policy and concerns. If the real rate of inflation is at 10% per annum or more the value of your capital will erode steadily.

Appreciation

Sometimes income is not the objective of the investment. Some investors may be looking for capital growth though their investment appreciating in value. The yield, or return, in these cases is received when the asset is sold. Real estate is often viewed as one such asset. The Indian stock market, on the other hand, has had a compounded annual growth rate (CAGR) of 13.67% for the fifteen years to 2015, making it the most profitable investment today.

When one approaches investment, one must be prepared to accept the basic home truth that there is no such thing as a perfect investment. Some may give high returns, but no safety. Some others will give low returns but your capital would be safer. Bank deposits, for example, are extremely safe. The return is, however, low. In short, in choosing an investment the investor will have to make his decision on which are the more important principles and then place his monies equitably.

Investor Categories

Investors can be placed in the following categories:

- Conservative.
- Enterprising.
- Speculative.

Safety is extremely important to the conservative investor. His objective would be to preserve his invested capital and earn an income from it. Conservative investors do not revel in the game of playing the markets. They would normally make an investment and retain it for some time.

An enterprising investor is one who is not particularly worried by risks. He usually takes some risks. His main aims are income and capital appreciation.

The speculative investor is a gambler. He takes risks and believes in buying and selling investments in order to earn money or capital appreciation. He is usually a man who is in a hurry and attempts to make as much as he can in as short a time span as possible.

It is possible to be a bit of each. One can divide one's investments into parts. Thus, one part could be used for speculative purchases — another could be used for conservative buying.

Kinds of Investments

This leads us to the kinds of investments that one can make. These can be broadly classified into the following groups:

- Very secure fixed income investments;
- Secure fixed income investments;
- Fixed income investments; and
- Equity shares.

We are deliberating not considering real estate and property here and are confining ourselves to the more popular and more liquid investment avenues.

Very secure fixed income investments are those that are very safe and yield a fixed dividend or return every year. As the return is often lower than the rate of inflation, the real value of the capital invested actually falls over times. A prime example is a deposit with a bank. These deposits are extremely safe.

Secure fixed income investments are those that pay a fixed return and are reasonably secure. They do bear the risk of economic downturns. Schemes floated by mutual funds are in this category. Several schemes guarantee a fixed return. However, the possibility exists of their not being able to provide this return in a depressed market.

Fixed income investments are those that give reasonable returns but are not necessarily very safe (although they can be). Debentures and corporate fixed deposits are considered fixed income investments.

Equity shares are the ordinary shares of companies. Investments in equity shares can be risky in that, should the company make losses or go through an economic recession, the value of the shares could plunge during such periods. Alternatively, if the company is going through a good time, the shares could soar too.

Equity shares can be sub-divided into:

- **Income Shares:** These shares do not appreciate in value much but the dividends paid on them are high. Consequently, there is usually a limit on how much these shares will grow.
- **Growth Shares:** The earning of growth shares is higher than those in the same industry. Consequently, their appreciation is higher. The income or returns will be low as the company would be reinvesting the bulk of their profits in the company in order for it to grow.

~

Chapter 2

~

Shares for Investment

What is a Share?

A share represents ownership, i.e. a share, in the assets of a company. If a company has issued 1,00,000 shares of ₹ 10 each at par, each holder of a share has ownership in that company in proportion to his share holding. Each share would represent ownership of 0.001% of the company.

As one of the owners of a company, a shareholder is entitled to a portion of the company's profits (or losses) to the extent of his holdings. This can be increased or reduced by buying or selling more shares.

A company is bound to keep its members, namely shareholders, informed about its performance. This is accomplished by distributing annual reposts to shareholders. As ownership of companies vests in shareholders, all important decisions are made by them. It is for this purpose that annual general meetings, special general meetings and extraordinary general meetings are held — to pass accounts, approve dividends, decide on mergers/sales of subsidiaries and elect directors. Shareholders exercise their votes at these meetings in proportion to their holdings.

Shares may be issued only to the amount authorized in the memorandum and articles of association of a company. The amount issued is known as the issued share capital and this can be lower than the authorized share capital as the total number authorized may not be issued. Issued shares may be partly or fully paid depending on how the company calls for the subscribed shares. The amount called up on a share is known as it's paid up value. When the full value is called up it becomes fully paid and the shareholder has no further liability.

Types of Shares

The types of shares are as follows:

1. Ordinary or Equity Shares

Ordinary shares or equity shares as they are commonly known, are normally issued with a face value of either ₹ 10 each or ₹ 100 each. In recent years many companies have reduced the face value to ₹ 1 each. The face value of the shares of some other companies is ₹ 2 each. This is to make them more affordable to buyers and to also make available more shares for trading. The holders of these shares are the real owners of a company. They bear the rights of ownership and enjoy its benefits. In a bad year when the company has made little or no profits, they receive no dividends. Conversely, in good times they receive large dividends and bonus shares. These shareholders are the ones entitled to vote and decide on company policy. In liquidation, they divide among themselves the assets left over after all others, including the preference shareholders, have been paid. They stand to lose their investment if there are no assets left after the others have been paid off. On the other hand, they stand to make a lot of money if the assets remaining are far in excess of their original investments.

2. Preference Shares

Preference shares are not frequently issued nowadays. They carry the right of a fixed rate of dividend and preferential treatment at the time the company is liquidated. Preference shareholders are to be paid prior to the payment of ordinary shareholders.

Preference shareholders do not have the right to vote at annual general meetings or decide on company policy.

3. Cumulative Convertible Preference Shares.

This category of shares was first introduced in 1985-86 by Mr. V. P. Singh when he was the Finance Minister with the intention of diversifying the market and reducing the dependence of the corporate sector or public financial institutions.

The shares are cumulative to the extent that they have a right to a fixed rate of dividend. If a company has not had sufficient profits, the right to the dividend continues and the dividend due will accumulate. Additionally, these are convertible to equity shares after a period of time generally between three years and five years.

These may be issued either to set up new projects, to finance expansions or diversification, to finance modernization and to raise funds for working capital requirements.

In effect a cumulative convertible preference share (CCP) is a fully convertible debenture with a lower interest rate.

~

Chapter 3

~

Classification of Shares

Shares may be classified into different categories. Each category is distinct from the other and they either attract or repel investors.

Some of the more common classifications are descended below:

Blue Chips

The term "blue chip" is derived from the game of poker in which blue coloured chips have the highest value. Among shares, blue chips are shares of established, profitable, dividend paying companies. Blue chip stocks are seen as a less volatile investment than owning shares in companies without blue chip status because blue chips have an institutional status in the economy. They are safe investments with reasonable certainty of regular dividends and long term growth. These shares are widely held. Their managements enjoy a good reputation.

In India, companies such as ITC, TCS, Asian Paints and Infosys Technologies are considered blue chips.

Widow's Shares

These are shares of fundamentally strong companies which can be bought and forgotten about as they are safe. They would rarely become worthless pieces of paper, or even fall drastically in value.

The companies are usually "true blue" and pay regular dividends. The phrase "widow's shares" was coined to suggest that even widows who had no exposure to the world of finance and were blissfully ignorant of its complexities could, with their eyes closed, purchase these shares and sleep easy — secure in the knowledge their capital is safe and that they would receive regular income.

Widow's shares pay a regular dividend though they are not as high as or as generous as the more flamboyant ones and are not given to tremendous volatility in the market. Their price does not soar or plummet but bears a steady course. They are usually categorized as "A" quality shares and listed in the forward section or group A of the stock exchanges.

I would add a word of caution. It's important to understand that even though at one time they may have been "widows shares," they may not always be. We live in an ever changing and dynamic world. Some companies that were considered very safe have not fared well for various reasons. Some like Tata Steel and Indian Hotels have suffered losses and have skipped dividends. Therefore, if you are an investor my advice is that it would be foolhardy to buy and forget a share believing in its intrinsic value. We live in turbulent times. Change is rapid and unpredictable. Always keep an eye on your investments.

Wishful Shares

Wishful shares are the shares of companies that are not doing particularly well. Investors or speculators buy these with the fond hope that the fortunes of the company would change. It may happen — or it may not. I know several people who, with wishful thinking, purchased the shares of a well known company that had not been doing well for sometime. Within three months of their purchasing these shares, the company announced improved results and the share price trebled.

In-Style Shares

These are shares of companies that people purchase as it is in vogue to purchase them and as one wishes to be "one of the gang."

Optimistic Shares

Optimistic shares are those that are expected to rise substantially in the short term. They are bought in expectation of great profits. One can make thumping profits — or thumping losses.

Low High Shares

These are low priced shares which the investor believes will rise in value at which time he could sell them at a profit. These are, in other words, low priced shares which appear to have the potential to rise in value.

Trading Shares

Trading shares are bought by investors in order to sell them at the earliest opportunity of making a certain profit. The companies may not be particularly strong but the shares have the potential of rising. The investor does not believe in holding these shares.

Sensitivity Shares

These are shares on which the movement of the market and the stock exchange index is calculated. These are usually "A" group shares. Their movement up or down determines whether the stock exchange sensitivity index rises or falls.

~

Chapter 4

~

Shares are for Everyone

Several years ago, in New York, a large money center bank sent out a questionnaire on investment objectives to a cross section of its depositors and clients. 89 per cent of those to whom it was sent replied. When evaluated the results were as follows — 43 per cent considered safety as the most important objective in choosing an investment, 34 per cent believed returns or yield was the most important consideration, while 18 per cent felt liquidity should be the deciding factor. Without doubt, all these reasons are important. The preference of the investment objective, however, will differ on the circumstances of an individual and his needs. Shares offer an individual the opportunity to opt for the objective of his choice and it is for this reason that shares are said to be for everyone.

Safety is undoubtedly an important investment objective. One works hard to earn and would like to invest and save for exigencies and old age. It is imperative that savings are not eroded and the risk of capital loss is low.

Return on investment is usually the measure that determines the success of an investment. How much has the investment appreciated and in relation to others? The aim is to obtain the highest return possible (dividend plus capital appreciation). Normally the rule is "the higher the risk the higher the return." It must also be ensured that the return is higher than the rate of inflation in order to protect the purchasing power of the investment.

Liquidity is necessary in case one needs money to meet unexpected expenditure or exigencies in a hurry.

Shares that meet these needs admirably are those of blue chip companies. They are extremely safe. The Nifty is the benchmark of the Indian stock market. The Nifty (National Stock Exchange Fifty) comprises of 50 large cap shares which are said to be India's blue chips. During the last 15 years to March 2015, these shares gave 511% absolute returns which works out to an annualised return of 12.3%. Some, such as HDFC and Asian Paints, gave returns in excess of 4,000%. This is many times the rate of inflation during this period. And shares can be converted into money quite easily as they can be sold freely on the stock exchange.

To determine the shares one should purchase, one's personal needs must be taken into account. Let us consider the following examples:

- Aditya Singh is a young executive. He is not married nor does he intend to marry for a few years. He is able to save about ₹ 10,000 per month. He would like to make this saving grow as rapidly as possible as he wishes to purchase a home of his own at the earliest.
- Vivan Daruwala is a family man. He has two sons in school. He would like to ensure that in ten years he has enough money to send his children abroad to study and to give them a start in life.
- Pradeep Nayar has a daughter who is in college. He has substantial savings. His main objective is to ensure that there is enough for him to marry his daughter off.
- In five years Rahul Mukherjee would be retiring from his salaried employment. He needs to ensure that his investments and savings yield him a return that would enable him to maintain a reasonable standard of living.

The needs of each of these individuals are different and this must be taken into account when their savings are invested.

Aditya Singh is young and without encumbrances. He lives with his parents and apart from spending on himself for his own pleasure has very few expenses. His savings represent to him capital for the future. As he needs to build capital, purchase a house and marry, he must invest his savings in shares which are likely to grow rapidly. He does not need income immediately and so he must aim at capital growth. The ideal investments for him would be new companies or slightly riskier companies as the potential for rapid growth is enormous. It is admitted though that there is a possibility of losses in investing in such companies but then Aditya is young and it is worth taking the risk.

On the other hand, Vivan Daruwala needs both growth and security. He has a family to look after and has to ensure that in a decade he has enough to send his children to college. He cannot afford any deterioration in his savings. His savings must appreciate. He does not require an income now. He could place about 50% of his capital in blue chips and the balance is shares of second tier companies so that there is no erosion in capital.

Pradeep Nayar has substantial savings and has probably enough to ensure that his daughter is properly married. His investments should be diversified in blue chips, medium risk and high risk shares in such a way that he gets both income and his investments appreciate in value. In order to protect his assets, at least 50 per cent of his assets should be in blue chips. This would ensure that his base is protected. Additionally, not more than 15 per cent of his portfolio should be in high risk shares.

As Rahul Mukherjee would be retiring in 5 years, his main objective has to be income. He should invest at least 30 per cent of his capital in blue chips. The balance should be in gilt or fixed income funds that would give him a regular income by way of dividends. This would ensure against deterioration in capital and give him a regular income.

These illustrations show how investment in shares can meet every need and there is a wide variety of shares to choose from.

~

Chapter 5

~

Why Invest in Shares

Rajiv Menon invested the entire gift of ₹ 100,000 that he had received from his father in shares. Gangadhar Bale borrowed ₹ 150,000 to purchase shares. The question that several individuals asked them was: "Why shares? Why not place the monies in mutual funds, fixed deposits or more conventional forms of investment and savings?"

Walter Gutman once said, "There is nothing like the ticker tape except a woman, nothing that promises hour after hour, day after day such sudden development, nothing that disappoints so often or occasionally fulfils with such unbelievable, passionate magnificence."

Investments in shares have an aura of speculation and buccaneering of large fortunes made and lost. Although there is an element of risk in investing in shares, there are several reasons for considering this avenue of investment.

Profits or Growth

Few other investments open to invdividual investors have the potential of growth comparable to shares and if purchased at the right time can yield impressive and incredible returns. During the last few years the top wealth creators have been given in Tables 5.1 and 5.2.

Table 5.1

The Fastest Wealth Creators between 2010–15

Company	CAGR %
Ajanta Pharma	119
Symphony	108
Eicher Motors	90
P I Industries	85

Table 5.2

The Most Consistent in 10 Years (2006-2015)

Company	CAGR %
Titan	43
Sun Pharma	36
Asian Paints	35
Kotak Mahindra	34
Dabur India	31

These shares listed in Table 5.1 and Table 5.2 have grown many fold. Investors who had the foresight to invest in these at the right time have reaped a fortune. Investment in shares has consistently rewarded Indian investors with a CAGR of 13%. This is better than any other investment available. In short, money invested in shares multiplies faster than other conventional avenues of investment savings.

Minimal Outlay

One does not require a lot of capital to purchase shares. Several shares are priced below ₹ 500 per share and hence one can begin a portfolio with an initial investment of as little as ₹ 25,000 to ₹ 50,000.

Liquidity

Investments in shares are extremely liquid. In India, one can now sell shares and receive the proceeds in a matter of days; earlier pre-dematerialization it took weeks. This is not possible in most other alternatives. In the case of bank deposits, for example, one would be compelled to pay a penalty (up to 1 per cent) for early encashment.

Decisions can be Changed

Decisions made are not irrevocable. If one purchases real estate it would be difficult to reverse it and sell it in a hurry without incurring a loss or a hefty tax. Shares can be sold easily and freely in the stock exchange as and when one desires.

Hedge Against Inflation

Shares are a tremendous hedge against inflation. Although the declared rate of Indian inflation is around 5%, the real rate of inflation is in the region of 9 per cent. This represents, it must be realized, the decline in the purchasing power of the rupee. Further more, the rate of inflation is higher than the interest received on bank deposits and other forms of savings or investment. Only shares have consistently yielded income and growth, over a period of time, that is significantly in excess of the rate of inflation. As mentioned earlier, the CAGR has been 13% during the last few years.

Safety

Unless one sinks one's money in an absolute dunderhole of a company, a lemon, one's investment is reasonably safe. And some are safer than the others. One will not lose "the proverbial shirt" if monies are invested in good, sound companies. This is why certain shares are known as widow's shares (Nifty 50 shares for example). Their reputation is such that it is suggested that one can purchase them and forget about them. They pay dividends regularly, issue bonus shares and the company would never go bust.

Wide Choice of Shares

Thousands of companies operating in different markets and diverse industries are quoted on the stock exchanges in India and one has a wide choice from which to choose.

Tax Advantage

The government has recognized the fact that to industrialize the nation it is important to channelize investments and savings to industry and the corporate sector and several tax benefits are therefore given for investments in shares. For example:

- Dividend income is not taxable in the investor's bank.
- Capital gains tax is not payable if the shares have been held for over a year.
- No wealth tax is payable on shares.

Collateral Facility

Several banks and other financial institutions lend money to individuals on pledging shares as collateral. This is extremely useful if the loan is required for a short term and one does not wish to part with the asset.

Ownership of a Large Enterprise

The ownership of a share gives the investor a part ownership in the company. Although s/he may not be able to wield the rights of ownership and determine policy and strategy with a 100 shares in Reliance or Infosys or Tata Motors, but s/he can attend annual and general meetings, vote, question the directors and inspect the books.

Thus, an equity investor directly contributes to the growth of the company and the country.

The Game

Finally investing in shares is also akin to a game. It is thrilling to watch the performance of the company one has invested in and the price of the share — its ups and downs. It is addictive to the extent that after one has purchased a share it is difficult not to check its price everyday. Hours can be spent on deciding whether to sell or to buy more. And the result is the realization of the decision — whether it was the correct one or not. It is exciting and fun. As the 16th century European De La Vega said "and once you have tasted the honey, you can never keep away from it."

~

Chapter 6

~

Personal Considerations for Investing in Shares

Once you decide to invest in shares, it is important that you determine:

- How much of your earnings you should invest in shares.
- The kind of shares that you should buy.

The decisions made on these would form the basis of an individual investor's investment strategy

How Much to Invest in Shares

How much of your earnings should you invest in shares? It is important that the funds you set aside to buy shares are those which are available after you have met your ongoing needs. Let us consider the case in Illustration 6.1.

Illustration 6.1

Satish Kohli is a salaried employee in middle management. He receives ₹ 1,37,000 every month after deductions. Out of this he spends ₹ 40,000 on food, ₹ 6,000 on society outgoings, ₹ 20,000 on children's education, ₹ 1,000 on life and medical insurance and another ₹ 20,000 on household expenses (electricity, telephone, clothes, etc. He has ₹ 50,000 left. Of this, he could use the entire amount or a

Contd . . .

Illustration 6.1 *(... contd)*

portion to purchase shares. In my opinion, it would be short-sighted to use one's entire disposable income to purchase shares because the possibility exists of large losses. In this instance, Mr. Kohli could invest, say, ₹ 30,000 in shares and keep the balance saved in other instruments, or for holidays and emergencies. In short, an individual should ensure that there is money saved or kept away for one's daily needs and for emergencies. Only that which is left over should be invested in shares.

What Kind of Shares Should You Buy

The shares that you purchase must depend on your risk level — the amount you are prepared to leave to chance. If you are prepared to gamble your entire savings on whether a dog will bark thrice or five times, you are obviously a born gambler and your capacity to take risks is extremely high. You are prepared to take large risks and make enormous gambles for windfall gains aware that you can lose your shirt should the gamble fail. The shares that you would purchase would be high risk shares which are extremely volatile. On the other hand, if you are concerned about the erosion of your capital then it would be wise to purchase safe shares — shares which do not appreciate or depreciate widely and pay reasonable dividends. It must be remembered, however, that risk and returns go hand in hand. The higher the risk, the higher the returns.

This, however, does not mean that only gamblers take risks. Level headed, careful people do take gambles too, but these gambles are often after careful consideration and this is what one should always remember if one is to be successful in investing in shares. Do not act on impulse. As Jean Paul Getty once said, "Do not buy the shares of a company until you know all about it." This is extremely important and cannot, I repeat, cannot be over emphasized.

Finally, you should also bear in mind the kind of return you are aspiring for because your portfolio will depend entirely on that. As a thumb rule the returns different types of investors can expect are indicated in Table 6.1.

The difference between the ultraconservative investor and the sheer gambler is the degree of safety they lay emphasis on. The conservative investor usually purchases a share and holds it for a period. His

Table 6.1

Returns Expected by Different Categories of Investors

Category of Investor	Desired Annual Return
Ultraconservative	3%
Cautious and conservative	5%
Careful	8%
Speculative	15%
Daredevil	25%
Sheer gambler	35% +

emphasis is on safeguarding his capital and the avoidance of losses. On the other hand, the speculator is keen on profits and short term gains. He does not mind taking chances. A blend between the two can yield very satisfactory results. To achieve this, one must know which shares to purchase, which companies to look at and the like, and this is why it is important to screen shares.

Priorities

The first thing you should do is to define your priorities. What is it you seek — is it capital appreciation, safety or income? It is this that you should determine which shares to buy and which not to buy. It is extremely important that you define these priorities because your entire strategy will have to be based on this. And the purchase of shares without a well defined strategy can be likened to a charging bull in a china shop. The result can only be a catastrophe.

~

Chapter 7

~

Share Selection

Prudent investment mandates that you must select the share you wish to purchase — whether it be for long term investment or for the short term. There are thousands of companies listed on the stock exchange and for obvious reasons, one cannot buy into them all, nor would one want to as many would obviously be "lemons," whereas others would be veritable "eagles and phoenixes." One needs to actually determine from this galaxy which ones are the "eagles" — the shares that will soar to Olympian heights, which are the ones that will be safe, and which are the shares that should be avoided.

Shares are purchased with the "Midas" objective in mind. "Midas" in this context does not refer to the mythical Greek king whose touch turned everything to gold, but is extended as follows:

M = Marketability.
I = Income.
D = Diversification.
A = Appreciation.
S = Security.

The decision based on the above fundamentals should be to select the right share in the right industry group that will fulfil your requirements.

In the process of choosing the shares that are right for you, the following factors will assist you.

Diversify Your Portfolio

The old adage "do not place your eggs in one basket" is an investment basic. If all one's funds are placed in one share or in one security and events take a downturn there could be a real catastrophe. To avert this possibility, it is always wise — I would even say mandatory — that one spreads one's investments, namely diversifies.

Type of Investment Spread

You should invest a portion of one's funds in real estate to ensure that you have a roof over your head. A portion should also be placed in safe investments like bank deposits or public sector bonds so that you receive some secure and stable income. Only the remainder should be invested in shares.

Industrial Spread

It is an accepted economic rule that every industry goes through a cycle of boom and then recession, depression and then a boom again. This happens for several reasons. At the time an industry is experiencing a boom, another may be going through a recession. Factors such as government policy, competition and such likes could also affect the performance of an industry. Consequently, it would be wise to limit one's investment in any particularly industry to, say, 15%. This is because if you are heavily focussed on an industry and the industry goes through an economic downturn, the value of the shares you own would plummet. There are several industries that are prone to downturns such as shipping, steel and the likes. There are also some that are evergreen like banking and pharmaceuticals. Investments in evergreen, shares can be higher. However, one should not forget the fact that some are extremely competitive such as pharmaceuticals as the companies in this industry are highly competitive and are only as good as the drugs they hold a patent to. In 2015, Dr Reddy which was doing extremely well lost over 40% of its market capitalisation as the FDA found flaws in ten of their factories.

Companies

Like industries, companies too go through periods of growth and setbacks. Metal Box was one of the most respected companies in India in the 1970s. A decade later, as a consequence of a disastrous diversification, the company was literally closed down. Similarly the fortunes of Peico (now Philips), after decades of excellent growth and profits, took a downturn in the 1980s. Reliance has grown to be one of the largest companies in India. So has Videocon — a company unknown in 1985. Infosys, promoted by professionals, is today among the most respected companies in the world. At its initial public offering, there were not enough investors and shares devolved on the underwriters. Thus, in order to safeguard against downturns a company may experience, it would be wise to limit one's investment in a single company to around 10% of the total, and upto a maximum of 12%. This will, to an extent, protect one against a major loss if one company goes under as one would hold shares in other companies too.

Location

It is also important to invest in companies in different locations, so that if some calamity occurs in one part of the country, companies in other locations will not be badly affected. Labour problems in West Bengal and Kerala have stunted growth in companies located there. Several companies have had to close down. The value of shares in these companies has fallen tremendously. In some instances the shares are practically valueless and are in many cases not marketable. To protect one's investments against such possibilities it is best to have shares in companies in different parts of the country.

It must always be remembered however, that diversifying your investments is not a guarantee against losses. It does, however, reduce the risk of large losses.

Prefer Diversified Companies

Diversified companies are those that produce different products. Also, their range of products or activity spans different industries. In India, for example, ITC is a diversified company. It is involved in tobacco, agribusiness, paper and hotels. So are Larsen & Toubro and

Hindustan Lever. It is also important to determine whether their products are market leaders. If not then a diversified company runs severe risks.

Apart from the desire to take advantage of an opportunity for growth and profits in another industry, the purpose of diversifications to safeguard the company and cushion a downturn should a depression occur in the industry the company is in.

Diversification has often helped companies through a difficult time. Indian textile companies that had diversified were able to ride the severe depression that all but wiped out the industry. Several others who had not diversified became "sick" companies. Diversification provides flexibility, security and stability to a company. Having said that it is important to ensure the company's products are market leaders. If they are not, the poor products can weigh the company down when the good products are going through a difficult time.

Additionally, diversification opens up new markets and new possibilities. Corporate history abounds with stories of companies purchasing other companies with different products to gain access to a new or wider market. For example, Citibank acquired the Diner's Club franchise in India in 1990. This immediately gave them access to new individuals to whom they could sell their other banking products. Of late, Indian companies have been buying companies abroad to gain access to new markets.

If the company's products are different and its factories are at different locations, a strike or a disaster in one factory will not usually affect other factories in other locations.

It must, of course, be accepted that during normal years single product, single factory and single market companies perform well. Their problems occur only when the industry swings into a recession or depression. They do not have the elasticity to weather such times.

One must be cautious while investing in non-diversified companies. There are exceptions, though. These are:

- Companies who enjoy a monopoly or a near monopoly. Till very recently, Indian car companies were in this enviable position.

- Companies which have captive markets for all that they produce. In India, it is still a seller's market in many industries. Fortunately, the number of such companies are reducing.
- Companies whose products are far superior to those of their competitors. Customers prefer to purchase such products even though they are more expensive.

However, situations can change and they are constantly doing so. It is advisable, therefore, to stay clear of one product, one market companies and to invest in well diversified ones unless a single product company is a clear market leader and professionally managed.

Choose Blue Chips

Strong, profitable, established and dividend paying companies are called "blue chips." Shares of such companies are safe investments and they yield regular dividends and appreciate in value with satisfying regularity. On account of the safety offered, the yield and appreciation is modest and less than other shares.

The Bigger the Better

The shares of larger companies are usually safer from an investment point of view as they are less prone to the vicissitudes of fortune and the turbulence of economic cycles. This is because:

1. Large companies are usually diversified and operate in many industries. Consequently, if one industry is in a depression, it would not be disastrous as its products in other industries may be doing well. Most large Indian companies are reasonably well diversified. They are, thus, less exposed to the vagaries of the economic cycle.
2. Bigger companies are usually multi-product and as a consequence their fate is not dependent on any single product.
3. As the factories and plants of larger companies are bigger, they are often able to take advantage of economies of scale. They can thus reduce the costs of production and optimise the use of the factors of production.
4. Large companies always attract the best talent as the growth opportunities, financial rewards and security they offer is greater.

They pick the crème a La crème of the graduates of the best educational institutions every year by actually going to campuses and recruiting the best. Additionally, they have the resources to train or send people on courses to improve their knowledge and enhance their expertise.

5. Large companies are often professionally managed. Professional managers are usually extremely sensitive to market conditions and are performance driven. They are constantly trying to improve upon their previous performance as their career often depends on it. And as performance is often judged not only by profits but by dividends and bonus shares issued, larger companies often tend to regularly reward investors by higher and regular dividends and with bonus issues.
6. Large companies have easier and better access to new technologies and possess better facilities for research.
7. Over the years larger companies have built up a tremendous amount of goodwill and the public have great trust in them. Any enterprise floated by a large group like the Tatas or Birlas are well supported by the public.
8. Obviously large companies started as small companies. The very fact that they are now large vindicates the fact that they are vibrant, dynamic and prosperous.
9. They have also greater access to capital. Banks are more comfortable lending to them and supporting their projects.

Having said this, what constitutes a large company for the purposes of investment? This is difficult to define. A simple yardstick to follow, without getting into arguments on what is and is not a large company, is that one should not invest in a company that has market capitalisation of lower than ₹ 5,000 crore.

Additionally, some other factors should also be looked at:

1. There should be a large number of shareholders.
2. The company should have a consistent record of profitability. Ideally, the average after-tax growth of profits should be around 20% p.a.
3. There should have been regular dividend payouts during the previous 3 to 5 years. Most Indian companies normally pay dividends of 20% or more.

4. The share price should have appreciated by about 25% to 30% per annum during the previous 3 years.
5. The company should have issued bonus shares periodically.

It must be remembered though that though there may be safety, the returns large companies pay are usually lower as they have a larger share capital to service.

Buy Low Price Shares

It is always wiser to buy low priced shares as the possibility of growth in the price of such low shares is much higher than in the case of high priced shares. Additionally, the loss that one may incur is much lower (*see* Illustration 7.1).

Illustration 7.1

Nikhil purchased 200 shares of a company in January 20XX at ₹ 750 per share. His total investment was ₹ 1,50,000. The price fell in December by a third to ₹ 500. Nikhil has a book loss of ₹ 50,000. Anand, on the other hand, had bought 2000 shares of another company at the same time for ₹ 75. This fell by ₹ 5 to ₹ 70 in December. On his investment of ₹ 1,50,000 he had a book loss of ₹ 10,000.

The scope for low priced shares to rise are high. This is why in recent times companies have brought down the face value of their shares from ₹ 10 to ₹ 5 or to ₹ 2 or even ₹ 1 per share. But then, that does not mean all low priced shares are good. Some prices are low because no one sees any potential for these companies. And some shares (like Infosys, HDFC, Wipro) are priced high because of their performance and their potential. One must examine the company whose share prices are low and if the fundamentals are good and it has potential, then one should buy the shares.

History Repeats Itself

One must always remember that history will repeat itself. Shares will rise, then fall, and rise again. Therefore, if there is a downturn in an industry it does not mean one should ignore those shares entirely. Those shares can rise again. Examples that readily come to mind include Larsen & Toubro, Reliance Industries, Mahindra and Mahindra and many others. One should realize that history repeats itself and share prices will rise and fall. One must aim to buy a share when it is at its low because it will rise. It is said, "Show me a man who does not believe in history and I will show you a fool."

Acting against the Tide

If one can act intelligently against the tide, the rewards can be very great. This effectively means purchasing shares when others are selling, or selling shares at a time when others are buying. The greatest benefit will occur if such contrarian action is taken just before the tide turns. A friend of mine bought Aarvee Denim shares at below ₹ 2 a share in 1993, at a time when the prices were depressed. He unloaded them in 2005 during the boom at ₹ 85. He was lucky.

To be successful in this one must be aware of market conditions — and also be lucky. Timing is all important as otherwise one can lose a considerable amount.

Watch for Volumes

Share prices rise or fall markedly when there are large purchases or sales. These occur when:

- There are large institutional purchases of shares.
- A large corporation or group is trying to corner the shares.
- A large number of shares are being off-loaded by a group or institution for liquidity in anticipation of a downturn in the company.
- Good news or increased profits are anticipated.

When share prices rise or fall sharply hold on for a while and investigate the reasons. Recently as a large financial institution needed liquidity immediately, it sold a major portion of its large holding in a company. As supply at that moment exceeded demand, the share prices fell. This was not to be construed as a reflection of the performance of the company and those who bought shares at that time when the prices fell are happy persons.

Volume and Price

When the volume of sales of a share increases, prices begin to fall as the supply exceeds demand. On the other hand, when the volume of purchases increases, prices rise as the demand exceeds supply.

This illustrates the basic economic law of supply and demand. However, when prices rise without a corresponding increase in the volume, it may be interpreted as someone managing or manipulating the price — to enable themselves to sell at a profit. Similarly if the shares fall in value without a rise in volume, it would be prudent to wait a while and figure out what's happening before selling.

Reverse Trend

Sometimes when most other shares are falling, the share of a company may be stable or even rise. Similarly, when the prices of most shares are rising, the share of a company may be falling. If the price of the share is falling in a rising market, it may be because the particular company is not doing well and it would be wise to get rid of it. As a general rule, if a share falls by over 12.5% (one-eighth) it would be prudent to get rid of it.

Correspondingly, if the shares rise in a falling market, the possibility exists that in time the price of these shares will also fall. Hence, as a rule it would be wise to sell a share, if its price rises by an eighth (12.5%).

Be Cautious of Smaller Companies

Small companies are more vulnerable. Often they are single product companies in the process of establishing themselves. At the start it is a struggle — finances are slim and facilities may not be adequate. Often the managers are young and inexperienced. In a period of depression or recession, as the resources and support that smaller companies get are slender, they often go under. Their mortality is much higher and bankers and financial institutions are usually not very keen to bail them out. Many collapse, therefore, when things go sour.

This does not mean one should never invest in smaller companies. Smaller companies grow to large companies and monies invested in small companies can multiply many times. IT companies are living examples of this. Nevertheless, many companies do not make it and their share prices remain depressingly low.

Realizing the inherent risks, one would be wise to consider some pointers while investing in smaller companies:

1. The parentage of the company should be looked at. If the company has been promoted by a well known group, the possibilities are that the parent company or group will support it.
2. Reputation of the management is important. Managements make or break a company. A company managed by a dynamic, innovative group of people would grow and prosper.
3. The prosperity of a company also depends on its products. If the products are in demand and their quality is good, sales will be high and will increase year after year.
4. The industry the company is in should also be considered. Is the industry prone to major reverses? Classic examples of such industries are shipping and textiles. Is the industry a sunrise, namely the fast developing one like the consumer goods or electronics industry, or a sunset industry, namely an industry that has grown and is about to fade away or go into a depression — a classic example is the jute industry.
5. The company's share price record should also be looked at. If there is a steady growth in price, it is an indication of stability.
6. The company's financials must also be examined. One should look for a steady growth in sales and profits every year and check whether a consistent trend can be perceived.
7. One should also check what the company does with its profits. Is the entire amount ploughed back into the company or is it entirely distributed to the shareholders? This is extremely important to determine whether the company will grow or not.
8. Additionally, it is always wise to speak to friends, colleagues, accountants or anyone else who may have heard or may know something of the company.

While this is not an exhaustive list, these are some of the things one should look at while considering the purchase of shares in a small company.

Be Wary of Closely Held or Family Controlled Companies

The term "closely held company" relates to those companies whose shares are not widely held by a large number of investors and are seldom traded on the stock exchange. The shares are usually held by a few individuals, often members of a single family. Consequently, there is not much demand for these shares and they are often difficult to sell. As a thumb rule, a company in which the promoter and his group hold over 70%, may be termed as closely held company.

The group or family that controls closely held companies usually has the majority stake in the company. Consequently, they make plans for the companies and determine policies with their interests in mind and without much care or concern for other shareholders. As far as they are concerned, the company is theirs. Here is how things work out in such companies:

- The group or family that controls the company has no interest in diluting their holding. Consequently, the shares are not regularly traded and there is no great demand for them.
- As there is no demand for the shares — the only person likely to want the shares being the controlling group or family — they can be difficult to get rid of. Others, aware of the difficulty in selling the shares, are not likely to be interested in purchasing them.
- The dividend payouts of closely held companies will be on the whim of the controlling group. Often, as they would be directors or employees of the company, they may charge the company large fees or salaries. As their own financial needs are met, they may prefer to plough back the profits into the business as opposed to distributing dividends. Thus, other shareholders may get little or no income.

  As little or no dividend is distributed and there is little demand for these shares, there is little scope of capital appreciation and these remain quoted at incredibly low rates for long periods of time. At times, the market value of such shares is even less than their actual book value — a phenomenon unheard of among widely traded shares.
- There is usually a dearth of information regarding closely held companies. Details of their working, their plans for the future,

their results and the like are not easily available. Consequently, one could get misled by their prospects.

- People who are groomed to take control of these companies are not executives who have given their lifeblood for the company, but the sons or daughters of the family. They may not be capable or competent but they are given the reins — often to the detriment of the company. There are, however, several instances in Indian industrial history that disproves this. There are also several who prove this contention. A positive factor today is that many scions of large industrial houses are spending time learning business techniques and theory and actually working on the shop floor to learn the "ropes" of the businesses they would one day manage. A conscious attempt is being made to be worthy of and aware of the company or entity.

This does not mean one should not invest in family controlled companies. In India today, many of the large prosperous companies are family controlled.

The point I wish to make is be wary. Consider the integrity and professionalism of the family before you invest in a company. Do not, however, invest in a closely held company because it would be extremely difficult to get rid of your investment, namely sell your shares when you want to and you will be at the mercy of the group that holds the controlling interest.

Do Not Invest in Unlisted Shares

A share is stated to be listed if it is traded in a recognized stock exchange. The quotes one sees in the business section of newspapers and magazines are details of the prices at which listed shares were traded in the exchange. A share can be listed in more than one exchange and can therefore be "listed" at different rates. This is because offers can differ from one market place to another and will rise or fall on the basis of the demand for or supply of the particular shares. Consequently, several sharp investors often buy a share at a market where the price is low and sell at another market where the price is higher, thus making a tidy profit. This is known as arbitrage.

The difficulty that one faces if unlisted shares are purchased is that they are not marketable. There is no market place where they can be offered for sale. These can only be sold in private deals to individuals who may want them for some reason and more often than not, they would have to be sold at a discount. Additionally, it is difficult to get information on unlisted shares. Companies whose shares are listed are required to publish quarterly and half-yearly results. Their performance and a huge array of historical performance statistics can be gleaned from newspapers, magazines, the Internet, etc. No such information is available usually on unlisted companies. As they are not duty bound to give this information, they do not give it.

On account of the lack of information on unlisted companies and the difficulty of selling their shares, it is advisable not to buy unlisted shares unless one proposes to take over the company. Then it does not matter if the shares are listed or unlisted.

It should be noted that listing on the stock exchange is optional and is done to make the shares marketable and provide liquidity. Additionally, listed shares have better standing with investors. However, to be listed, a company has to follow certain rules. It must disclose details of dividends, issues of capital, dates of closure of books and publish accounts periodically. Additionally, only those companies which offer at least 60% of their issued share capital to the public are eligible to be listed.

Avoid Inactive Shares

Shares are bought and sold everyday in the stock markets. However, not all shares are sold or bought and there may not be any transaction in several shares for considerable periods of time. Such shares are known as inactive shares.

How does one define an inactive share? For that matter — what is an active share?

- A share that is regularly traded is an active share.
- A share that is traded at least once a week can be termed as a reasonably active share.
- Shares that are traded only once a month are known as inactive shares.

- Shares that are not traded even once a month are known as slow moving inactive shares.

Now, these are not standard definitions by any means, but are groupings for convenience to differentiate the trading activity of a share.

Because they are inactive and there is little demand; inactive shares are usually available at a low price. At times, price flares up when there is some interest in the industry or the company is the subject of a takeover bid. But these could be momentary flashes and one should resist purchasing them simply because of the low price is not necessarily a bargain. Many shares are low priced because no one wants them.

Shares become inactive because no one wants to purchase them. This very fact itself should warn one against these shares. Often there may be many sellers but no takers — the basic situation of supply exceeding demand. This is why the shares are low priced. This situation also suggests that the general public would like to get "out of the share." No one wants it. Then why would you?

Do Not Invest in Companies with a Poor Industrial Relations Track Record

When trade unions become stronger and more militant, strikes and demands for higher pay and better conditions become more commonplace. These often lead to prolonged disputes, fall in productivity and even lockouts. These are to the company's detriment.

All companies have minor and occasional disputes with labour and these can lead to strikes. If these are few and far between, there is not much to worry. One needs to begin worrying if the strikes are frequent and recurring.

Companies that do have bad industrial relations suffer from low productivity, often poor quality products and general unrest. Consequently, profits are low and there are, at times, losses. It is unwise to invest in such a company, as one may not receive dividends and if the company is declared "sick" dividends may not be declared and the shares may not appreciate. Therefore, one should not invest in such companies unless one is certain that industrial relations will improve.

Avoid Vulnerable Companies

All persons are not equal. Similarly all companies are not equal. Even though they exist in the same country and share the same socio-political and economic concerns, their problems are not the same nor are their prospects the same. This is because some of these companies may be in an industry that is just developing (sunrise industry). Profits and sales gallop. On the other hand, in industries such as jute, profits have been steadily decreasing. Some industries are more vulnerable than others — the classic examples, of course, being shipping and textile. A company that is involved in cyclical industries sees its fortunes swing like a violent pendulum. Prices rise and fall with frightening regularity. It is safer to be away from such companies.

Cut Your Losses

If the shares you have bought are falling in price, the general tendency is to hold on. No one wants to book losses and at the back of one's mind there is both hope and belief that the prices will bounce back. Frequently, they do not.

As a strategy, it is wise to sell if the price of share bought falls by 12.5% or more. One can always buy it back later if the price improves, or if the price falls further.

Buy Low, Sell High

Once when the legendary JP Morgan was asked by an investor, which share would go up and which would go down, he looked at him sternly in the eye and said, "Son, it will fluctuate." This is very true. Prices will go up and down. The aim of every investor should be to buy the shares when the price is low and sell them when they become high.

Investing in Sick Companies

It is foolish and foolhardy to buy shares of sick companies as it would take a long time (if ever) for the company to begin making profits and pay dividends and, during that time, the investment will earn no returns at all.

Sick industries can turn a round and begin making profits. Sometimes sick companies are taken over because of their accumulated profits. When that happens, prices will rise and the investment will be very profitable if the shares are purchased before the "news" becomes public.

Do Not React on Sudden Rises or Falls

Sometimes shares may rise suddenly in a very short period. This surge is usually in anticipation or the happening of an event. At this time, one should not buy because after the surge, the prices may fall a little and then stabilize. It is better to wait till the shares stabilize. Similarly, share prices may fall very fast very soon. Often when taxes are increased, as a reaction even before the effect of the higher taxes are assessed, there may be a fall in the prices of certain shares. This is the result of the initial reaction to the news. For example, in December 2006 when the Governor of the Reserve Bank announced an increase in the cash reserve ratio of 0.5%, shares fell in three sessions by 1,000 points. After such sudden falls, prices typically rally back and settle at a higher price.

Investing in Laggards

Laggards are companies which are not performing well — companies that are only making small profits, if at all. Usually they have been incurring losses for years. This may be for diverse reasons — depression in the industry, bad management and the like.

Investing in these companies are risky as the shares would be depressed and there will always be the possibility of the laggard turning sick. Additionally, the investor will not get any returns on these shares. However, there is the probability and the possibility of a laggard turning around and making profits; of laggard merging with or being taken over by a profitable company. In such circumstances, the price will soar. The investor stands to make a lot of money if he buys the shares prior to the event or before others become aware of it. I state this because as soon as good news, or for that matter bad news, are even rumoured, the stock exchange gets wind of it and share prices react.

~

Chapter 8

~

How Shares are Bought and Sold

How does one purchase or sell shares in the open market? If you wanted to buy, say, 500 shares of Infosys, how would you acquire them? Or, if you wished to sell 1,000 shares of Unilever whom would you dispose of those shares to? Of course, you could search around for someone who wished to sell 500 shares of Infosys and purchase them or find someone who wished to buy 1,000 shares of Unilever. On a practical level this may be difficult and even if there are such people you may not be able to find them. Stock exchanges or markets came into being as a place where buyers could purchase what they wanted and sellers could sell the shares that they wished to be rid of.

The stock exchange is a market where securities are bought and sold. However, unlike usual markets all sellers and all buyers do not visit it but deal through their agents who are members of the stock exchange. This makes the operations more controlled, disciplined and workable. Earlier there were brokers and jobbers. Brokers brought and sold on behalf of their clients. Jobbers were intermediaries who dealt with specific shares. Brokers approached them if they wanted to buy or sell a share. With computerisation and online trading, jobbers have ceased to exist.

If an individual wishes to invest in shares, he must first open an account with a depository participant. This is because all shares that are traded have been dematerialised and are held in depositories. The individual must then also register himself with a broker.

A stock market is like an auction house. Buyers offer a price and if the seller is agreeable to the offer a transaction is completed. Buyers naturally try to purchase at the lowest rate and the seller aims to sell his holdings at the highest price.

How does the procedure take place? Vijay Rao wishes to buy 500 shares of Company A. He would place with his broker an order for the purchase stipulating usually the maximum price he is prepared to go up to. The broker would punch the order into the NSE system or BSE system (known as BOLT). Others who are keen on selling the share would also punch in the price they would like to sell at. As soon as prices match, the deal is consummated.

The first thing a prospective buyer or seller has to do is to locate a broker. This can sometimes be difficult especially if one is new to the city and does not know anyone. In those situations one can ask his bank manager or a business colleague for an introduction. Ideally one should deal with a registered stock broker (an actual member of the stock exchange) as he is obliged to fulfil every contract that he enters into whether it be for a purchase or a sale. If he does not, the stock exchange authorities can take action against him, debar him from membership and take other measures.

Often, however, a large busy broker may not be interested in acting for a small investor and this is not an uncommon occurrence these days. It may be necessary then to deal with a sub-broker operating under a registered broker. There is a little danger in dealing through sub-brokers. Since sub-brokers are not members of the stock exchange, disputes or disagreements between an investor and his sub-broker does not fall under the regulatory control of the exchanges.

Once having zeroed in on a broker, one must discuss the commission he proposes to take. The maximum commission that can be charged is 2.5% but there is no minimum. On an average commissions are between ½ per cent and 1 per cent. The percentage will depend really on the need of the broker for your business and your trading volume. However, when you buy a share, it would not be apparent as to what the commission is that the broker has taken because the price quoted is, say ₹ 201 net to you. If your agreement was a commission of ½ per cent, the actual sale price in this instance would be ₹ 200 per share and the broker's commission would be ₹ 1.

Now having settled this how do you instruct your broker? You have two options.

- You could ask the broker to purchase or sell from the "market." This means that you are authorizing your broker to buy from the stock market at the ruling market price. One normally places such an order when the market is going up or it is expected that the price of the share will rise.
- You can instruct the broker with limits, i.e. to purchase a share at a maximum of ₹ 255 per share or to sell at not less than ₹ 258 per share. You could tell him that if the shares are not currently available or cannot be sold (as applicable) at the price stipulated that he should not take any action and conversely he should get back to you. One would do this when:
    1. The markets are reasonably stable and a large or dramatic rise in prices is not anticipated.
    2. One is cautious and wants to control his commitments.
    3. One is unprepared to give *carte blanche* to one's broker.
    4. One does not expect to make a large profit and therefore does not want to buy at a very high price.
- On receiving your instruction, the broker would punch in the quantity and the rate into the system. When a match takes place the deal is consummated.

Normally if a broker is unable to execute the contract during the day then it usually lapses. Orders have to be given fresh every day. This is because the market is volatile and can fluctuate enormously. And it is important that one does not give orders without any time limits because it is possible that on account of bad news, calamities and the likes the price may plunge.

Another way a person could purchase or sell a share is by online trading. One can register with companies such as Kotak Securities or Share Khan and buy or sell shares without the intervention of a broker. I do not recommend this for the beginner because it is possible to make mistakes if one is not familiar with what to do.

At times a broker may himself own the shares his client wishes to buy or he may wish to buy the shares his client wishes to sell. In these instances if the transaction one does go through it is called a trade "from principal to principal."

The relation between clients and brokers are determined by the laws of the stock exchange where the broker is registered. The broker is personally liable to third parties for any transactions he enters into on behalf of his clients. Consequently the broker is entitled to, if the client does not honour his commitment to pay for the shares purchased, claim any loss he has incurred as a consequence from his client.

The question that would immediately arise is what protection is offered to a client if a broker defaults A client can, after serving a written notice to the broker, settle his contracts through another broker. He can then claim any loss that he has incurred. He can also complain to the governing body of the exchange The board is obliged to investigate the complaint and if the broker is found to be guilty to take suitable action. In extreme cases the broker would be declared as a defaulter. The defaulter committee would take into custody his books of account, papers and securities. This committee would then sell the members assets (including shares) and take custody of his money and distribute them pro rata between the other members. As is usual in such cases, the claims of the clients would be considered last. Consequently the small investor is at a disadvantage. To protect clients and small investors an insurance fund has been created.

As a last option clients can seek redress from civil or criminal courts. This is however, time consuming and costly and should be only a last resort.

There are a few points that should be remembered and are worthy of comment:

1. In choosing a broker it is always preferable to select one who is recommended by someone who has dealt with him for sometime and is satisfied with his integrity and honesty.
2. Brokers often give advice. This in itself is good but before you act on this advice it is prudent to remember that the broker may have a vested interest in the advice that is doled out. There may be a share he is unable to sell at a particular price. It is therefore always better to check with one or two others before the order is given.
3. A common complaint that most buyers have is that the broker appears to have purchased the share at the highest price for the day and sold them for the lowest price for the day. This is not really true as soon as an individual's order is punched in it is given a number is derived and the time of booking the order is made.

Chapter 9

~

Futures and Options

Alan Greenspan, former Chairman, Board of Governors of the US Federal Reserve once said, "By far the most significant event in finance in the past decade has been the extraordinary development and expansion of financial derivatives. These instruments enhance the ability to differentiate risk and allocate it to those investors most able and willing to take it — a process that has undoubtedly improved national productivity growth and standards of living."

The intent of any investor is to maximize returns and reduce risks. Derivatives are contracts that were created to minimize risks.

Futures and options are derivative products that can be traded on the exchange. These were first introduced in India in 2000 — the first trade being done on 9 June 2000.

Futures

A futures contract is a contract to buy or sell a specific security at a future date at an agreed price. The holder has both a right and an obligation.

Options

An option gives the holder the right but not the obligation to buy (call option) or sell (put option) something on or before a specified date at a stated price. The purchaser of the option pays a one time non-refundable fee (option premium) to the option seller (writer).

An investor can purchase or sell both index based and stock based options and futures.

When the purchaser exercises the option, he either pays the agreed or strike price if it is a call option or receives payment if it is a put option. If the option holder waives his option, he loses the option premium. On the other hand, the writer cannot waive and is obligated to make or receive delivery.

Futures and options are based either on the index or specific stocks. The investor has the choice of either investing on how the index is likely to move or on a specific share.

Index

The market is represented by an index. An index is made up of various shares from different sectors that trade in the market. Each share has a certain weightage in the index and depending on the movement of these stocks, the index goes up or down. There are several indexes, the most popular being the Bombay Stock Exchange Sensitivity Index known as the Sensex.

Index Futures

An index future is a contract entered into on the future of the index. There is no underlying security that has to be delivered to fulfil the terms of the contract. These are settled in cash.

Let us assume the Sensex is 25,000. You believe that the index will rise further. You enter into a contract to buy 100 units. The initial margin is 10%. The investment made would therefore be ₹ 2,50,000. Every buyer needs a seller. Let us assume that Mr. Ram believes the market will go down. Mr. Ram enters into a contract to sell a similar amount. He would also pay a margin of 10%, i.e. ₹ 2,50,000.

Everyday the index future is marked to market. This means that if the price falls, the purchaser has to pay the difference in margin money to the broker who in turn passes it on to the seller.

If on the last day the Sensex is 27,000, the buyer would receive the deposit of ₹ 2,50,000 plus the increase (27,000 less 25,000) multiplied by the number of units purchased.

If however, the index has fallen, then the person would have to bear the loss.

Index Options

Index options give the right but not the obligation to buy or sell the index at a future date. These are also cash settled. Generally these are European Style. This means that the right can be exercised only on the expiration date. The indices for the index option are those that are permitted by the exchange.

Stock Futures

A stock future is a contract to buy or sell a specific stock at a future date at an agreed price. Single stock futures are cash settled.

It must be remembered that when you buy a share, you pay the market price of the share (and the commission to the broker) and become a part owner of the company. When you buy a futures contract, you enter into a contract. No money is paid other than the commission to the broker. You will also need to pay a certain amount of margin (around 10%) as good faith to cover possible losses. If the share falls in price, the contact would have lost value and the broker would advise you that your unrealized losses have gone beyond minimum margin requirements. This is called a "margin call." If the margin call is not met, the broker has the right to liquidate your position.

The benefit of entering into a futures contract is leverage — the ability to purchase more. Let us assume you have ₹ 100,000. The shares of Nivya Ltd. are trading at ₹ 200 each. If you buy the shares outright, you will be able to purchase 500 shares. If the margin on these shares 50%, you will be able to purchase futures of 1,000 shares. If the price rises by 10% your profit if you had entered into a futures contract would be ₹ 20,000. On the other hand, if you had purchased outright, the profit made would be only ₹ 10,000.

Stock Options

Stock options are options contracts where the underlyings are individual stocks. These contracts are usually cash settled and are American Style. This means that the option can be exercised on or before the expiration date.

If an investor believes the price will rise, he'd buy a call option. On the other hand, if it is believed the price will fall, a put option would be purchased. The premium or discount for each option reflects what the market feels (*see* Illustration 9.1).

Illustration 9.1

Let us assume that an investor has shares of ABC Ltd., which are trading at ₹ 2,800 in April 200X. Three month options of ABC Ltd. are traded on the exchange at ₹ 3,000. This gives the owner the right to buy (call) shares at ₹ 3,000 (exercise price) upto 30 June, 200X. If the share price of ABC Ltd is less than or equal to ₹ 3,000, the contract is useless to the owner and he would lose the money he paid to buy the option (the premium). However, the premium is the maximum amount the owner can lose. The loss is thus limited. If however, the price of ABC Ltd. advances to ₹ 3,400, the owner of the call option can exercise the contract, buy the shares at ₹ 3,000 and sell it at the market price of ₹ 3,400. There is no limit to the upward gain that can be made.

Monthly and Weekly Options

Originally, equity futures and options were introduced in India with a maximum life of 3 months. These options would expire on the last Thursday of the expiring month. As the market felt that there should be options of a shorter maturity, weekly options were introduced in September 2004. Weekly options are similar to monthly options except that they are settled on Friday every week. Weekly options can be either for a week or for two weeks. Weekly options expire on Fridays. Weekly options have lower premiums than monthly options as they are of a shorter maturity.

~

Chapter 10

~

Public Issues of Shares

During the late 1970s and the early 1980s, many companies were floated and offered for sale to an eager public. Several were new and others (though old) were privately held, such as the Godrej companies. At that time, the Indian individual investor was, as a consequence of several FERA dilutions, becoming aware of the tremendous potential of the share market and eager to claim his share of the bounty. Issues oversubscribed by over 50 times were so common that they passed un-remarked and to an extent unnoticed. Such was the craze that nearly all public issues closed at the earliest date permitted — several being oversubscribed on the day of opening itself. When listed for trading the shares were often quoted five or six times their market value and many a wily investor took home the large rewards that resulted.

After the Harshad Mehta scam and then later after the Ketan Parekh scam there were very few new issues floated. That changed with the economy prospering after 2004 when there were several new issues. These were oversubscribed significantly and all, bar a few, quoting at impressive premiums. However, as a consequence of the global meltdown in 2008, retail investors fled the market badly bruised and it was only after the election of a new government in 2014 in India and the euphoria that followed that retail investors began limping back to the market.

Between April and December 2015 roughly ₹ 11,000 crore was raised through initial public offerings. The fact the investor had grown discerning is apparent from the price these shares quoted at after the public offer; now quoting at a discount and the appreciations of a few are not huge (*see* Table 10.1).

Table 10.1

Initial Public Offerings from April–December 2015

Company	Offer price (₹)	Market Price Dec 2015 (₹)	Return %
Adlabs	168	114.80	(31.67)
Manpasand Beverages	320	424.40	32.63
Syngene International	250	360	44.00
Power Mechanical Project	640	614.25	(4.02_)
Navkar Corporation	155	207.60	33.94
Shree Pushkar Chemicals and Fertilisers	178	160	(10.11)
Prabhat Dairy	115	142.80	24.17
Coffee Day Enterprises	328	272.20	(17.01)
Interglobe Aviation	765	1184.15	54.84
S.H. Kelkar	180	217.50	20.83

Public Issues, whether initial or follow-on public offers were earlier the most popular manner of shares acquisition as the Indian investing public believed that they were getting the shares at a cheaper price.

When a company offers its shares to the general public to subscribe to, they are known as public issues. There are two kinds of issues:

1. **Offer by an existing company:** An existing company may offer its shares to the public when in need of capital for expansion, diversification, modernization or for working capital finance.
2. **Offer by a newly floated company:** Newly floated companies offer their shares to secure funds. Public issues are popular as the shares are priced very attractively. Shares are offered at a range (based on a study of how much is likely to be offered). Retail investors are expected to bid at the higher price. Later, when all the bids have come in and the shares are fully subscribed for, the company decides the price at which the shares should be priced.

The public subscribe to these shares in the belief that the prices will rise and that a profit will be made. However, although this is true in many cases, it would be wise to remember:

- Often, existing companies artificially pump up the price of their shares rise before a public issue in order to make the offer attractive. After the issue is over the share prices fall to their true value and it is not inconceivable for that price being even below the offer price.
- The possibility always exists of one not being allotted any shares in such a case. As a consequence, the investor loses interest on his money for a month or more. Even then most investors believe that it is still worthwhile to subscribe as the potential of great profits (if shares are allotted) exist.

A lot of the concerns an investor may have has been taken away by the rigorous checks done by SEBI before a share is permitted to be offered for sale to the public.

A great attraction of subscribing directly to public issues is, of course, the fact that one eliminates the middleman — the broker. There was, at one time, the hassle of not being allotted a share and not getting the refund due. Now, with the refunds being directly credited to one's account, there is no real issue.

Another reason for public issues being popular is that it enables small investors to enter the market easily.

In short, public issues are attractive as they enable investors to purchase shares at attractive rates.

Book Building

Book building is the capital issuance process used in initial public offers (IPO) which helps to determine price and demand. SEBI guidelines defines book building as "a process undertaken by which a demand for the securities proposed to be issued by a body corporate is elicited and built-up and the price for such securities is assessed for the determination of the quantum of such securities to be issued by means of a notice, circular, advertisement, document or information memoranda or offer document."

Book building is a process used in IPOs for efficient price discovery. It is a mechanism where, during the period for which the IPO is open, bids are collected from investors at various prices, which are above or equal to the floor price. The offer price is determined after the bid closing date.

As per SEBI guidelines, an issuer company can issue securities to the public through prospectus in the following manner:

- 100% of the net offer to the public through book building process.
- 75% of the net offer to the public through book building process and 25% at the price determined through book building. The fixed price portion is conducted like a normal public issue after the book built portion, during which the issue price is determined.

The concept of book building is relatively new in India. However, it is a common practice in most developed countries.

Public offers have to be open for a minimum of five days. During this period, the share is offered between a price band, e.g. ₹ 100 and ₹ 130. The lower price is known as the floor price. Investors and institutions are asked to bid between the two prices but not below the floor price. They can revise their offer before the issue closes. Retail investors are expected to bid at the higher price. After the closing date, based on the offers received, the issue price is determined and allocation of securities is made to the successful bidders.

Difference between Book Building Issue and Fixed Price Issue

In book building, securities are offered at prices above or equal to the floor prices, in case of a public issue whereas securities are offered at a fixed price. In case of book building, the demand can be known every day as the book is built. But in the case of public issue the demand is known at the close of the issue.

Factors to be Considered

New companies do have a high mortality.

Many new companies have tremendous potential and do extremely well while many others will not. One must attempt to differentiate between the two and should restrict application to only those that do have a future.

How does one judge this?

1. Product

The company's product or service is the first thing one should look at. What does the company to produce or service that it offers? Is it likely to be popular? When Videocon Appliances was floated in the end of 1980s, there was tremendous demand for its shares as Videocon had proven itself as a manufacturer of quality appliances and consumer durables. The products that were going to be manufactured were in answer to a perceived demand. If investors are unsure of the likely demand for and popularity of the product to be manufactured, the issue will not be very successful. In the recent past Power Grid Corporation, Credit Analysis and Research, Engineers India, Wonderla Holidays and Interglobe Aviation have also been successful as their product / service has been perceived to be good. On the other hand, several others did very badly because they were highly priced (Coffee Day Enterprises) or lacked public awareness.

While looking at the product or service, one should examine the need that will be there, its likely popularity, the location of the plant and the competition it is likely to face. In 1981 when Vam Organic was floated, there was no other manufacturer. The company enjoyed a virtual monopoly and did extremely well. On the other hand, in the early 1980s, dozens of leasing companies were floated. The first few were greeted with enthusiasm. Later, the reception was lukewarm and at times cold. Many of them closed down.

2. Promoter

Another very important factor one has to examine is who the company promoters are? Who is actually behind the company? The list of directors may read like a roll of honour of Indian industry. They may be eminent professionals and industrialists — men of proven competence and known for their successes. But these individuals may only be fronts — fronts for others who are the actual promoters. When looking at the promoters, one should look at their integrity and ability. The past can be a good indicator. If the same promoters had floated successful products and companies in the past, there is a good probability that the one being launched would also be successful.

3. Gestation

Very few companies begin making profits immediately. The issue is usually to raise funds to build the installation and purchase machinery and the likes. These take time. Additionally, there can be shortages of certain materials, delay in delivery which may result in the facility not opening on the date scheduled. Such delays could also result in higher costs and these higher costs, if unchecked, can threaten the economic viability of the company. At the time one is applying for shares in new companies, it would be extremely prudent to check from the prospectus issued by the company what it proposes to do with the monies collected and when commercial operations are likely to commence.

Additionally, it should be remembered that projects that have a long gestation period may be commissioned at a downturn in the economy and this could result in the company going deep into red. One should therefore choose, whenever possible, companies with a short gestation period

4. Share Capital

It would be wise to examine how big the equity base of the company would be. If the equity base is small, then in profitable conditions the profits distributable to the shareholders will be high. Conversely, if the base is wide, the profits distributable to shareholders will be low.

5. Tax Benefits

It is important to also examine the tax benefits available, as the tax component can really eat into the profits. The industrial undertaking if it is in a backward area, may be eligible for incentives like subsidies, tax holidays backward area reliefs and the like. Machinery purchase would be entitled to depreciation. Additionally, investors are entitled to reliefs under the Income Tax Act. Dividends received are tax free.

Chapter 11

~

Other Ways of Acquiring Shares

The other ways of acquiring or receiving shares are by way of:

1. Bonus issues;
2. Preferential allotment;
3. Rights offers; and
4. Others.

Bonus Issues

The announcement of a bonus share issue is eagerly awaited and always greeted with euphoria. There is excitement. Prior to this there is great speculation and this tends to increase the market price.

What are bonus shares? Bonus shares are shares issued free of cost to existing shareholders in proportion to the shares they already own. For example, in 2015 many companies issued bonuses — the notables being Infosys Technologies, Tech Mahindra, HCL Technologies, Aurobindo Pharmaceuticals, Kotak Mahindra and Colgate. Most of them offered one share for every share held. Therefore, if your holding was 500 shares, your holding would rise, after the bonus issue to 1,000 shares.

Bonus shares are issued to shareholders as on a particular date. They cannot be renounced. Similarly there is no question of delays, over subscription or under subscription as they are issued free of cost. Bonus shares cannot however be issued to company employees, debenture holders, depositors, directors or business associates.

Bonus issues don't really change the pattern of ownership as they are allotted to shareholders in proportion to the shares they already own. The number of shares in circulation would increase but there will be no change in the percentage of shares controlled by the individual or corporations.

For example, prior to the issue of 3 bonus shares for every 5 shares held, the ownership pattern of shares of Pura Ltd. was:

	Shares held (No.)	Percentage
Divya	400	40
Nikhila	250	25
Anand	150	15
General Public	200	20
Total	1,000	100

After the bonus issue, the holdings would be:

	Shares held (No.)	Percentage
Divya	640	40
Nikhila	400	25
Anand	240	15
General Public	320	20
Total	1,600	100

It would be evident from the above example that though the number of shares owned by an individual increased, the percentage of shares owned in the company did not change. As a result, there really is no reason why the issue of bonus shares should be greeted with such jubilation as it does not give the shareholder an additional advantage. However, rationality does not always prevail. It is presumably because the shareholder feels that his investment is better and the value of his investment has risen because he has got an additional share certificate.

Furthermore, the public are interested in bonus shares and the reasons for this leading to an increase in the market price are as follows:

1. Companies rarely reduce their rate of dividend. As a consequence usually even after the bonus issue the dividend declared would be the same. As a result dividend income to the shareholder increases.
2. After the issue of bonus shares, the prices (except in unusual circumstances) would not normally fall in proportion to the bonus issue. Samudra Ltd.'s share price is ₹ 102 cum bonus. On a 1 for 1 bonus being issued the price would not normally fall to ₹ 51/- It is more likely to be around ₹ 60. As a consequence a shareholder will make some money on these shares should he sell them.
3. Bonus issues are made by capitalizing existing reserves. It thus does not disturb the total of the shareholders' funds — only its composition. It is usually issued to broaden or increase the equity base — the shareholders' commitment to the company. As higher dividends too have to be paid, the issue of bonus shares have been held to be an indication of the Directors' belief that the future is bright.
4. A holder of bonus shares has a tax advantage for the calculation of capital gains tax on the sale of bonus shares. The Supreme Court has held that bonus shares do have a cost. This cost is to be calculated by arriving at an average price based on the original cost. Sanjeev purchased 500 shares of Pura Ltd. for ₹ 12 per share. A year later Pura Ltd. issued one bonus share for every one share held. The original investment would remain at ₹ 6,000 but the number of shares held would be 1,000. The average cost is therefore ₹ 6 per share. This would be the value of a bonus share for capital gains tax purpose not NIL (even though no amounts were paid). It must be remembered the cost of the original shares would remain unaltered at ₹ 12 per share for capital gains tax purposes.

There are conflicting judgments on the method of valuation if shares (original purchase plus bonus) are sold together. To avoid this it would always be more advisable to sell them separately.

There are some useful pointers regarding companies that do issue bonus shares:

1. Bonus shares are issued by companies that are growing and who have ploughed back a significant amount of profits back into the business. The value of the shares of these companies is based on the earnings per share.
2. If the dividends are maintained at the same rate as prior to the bonus issue, it suggests that the company believes its income will continue to be adequate and will grow.
3. By issuing bonus shares companies conserve cash (otherwise they may have to pay cash dividends). The cash conserved can be ploughed back into the company.
4. Bonus shares keep the price of shares at a reasonable level and thus keep them within the reach of small and medium investors. A high price may not attract these investors.
5. By making bonus issues a company can maintain a uniform dividend rate.

Preferential Offers

A preferential offer is one when a company offers shares in that company or a company that is its associate or subsidiary to a preferred group — usually to its shareholders or its promoter group. It is in effect a reward to the shareholders for their faith in the company as the shares are usually offered at a very attractive price. Hindustan UniLever several years ago offered its shareholders a preferential allotment of 40 shares of Lipton Ltd. for every 100 shares of Hindustan UniLever held at its face value of ₹ 10 per share. These shares were quoted at ₹ 72 at the time in a depressed stock market — giving the allotees an appreciation of 720% — a phenomenal amount.

Preferential offers of shares are attractive because:

1. They are usually offered at a very attractive price and there is reasonable certainty that the shares will appreciate within a reasonable time.

2. They are often offered at a price much lower than the ruling market price and the investor has the opportunity of selling the shares immediately after allotment thereby making a quick profit.
3. The investor in a preferential offer is guaranteed a minimum number of shares. He has a firm allotment and this removes considerably the anxiety of "will I, won't I be allotted a share" worry. As he has a firm allotment his money will not be returned with a letter of regret and loss of interest. He will get something.
4. Preferential offers to finance a new industry or company being set up enables the investor to get tax benefits in several cases.

One should remember that an investor is not under any obligation to subscribe to a preferential offer. One should study not only the details of the company whose shares are being offered but also its project, its viability and the likes, plus the mother company. The strength of the new company will always be the mother company and if the mother company is strong and if the project fails, the mother company will more often than not come to the rescue. Tata Chemicals floated Tata Fertilizers. As the project did not take off as expected, Tata Chemicals took over Tata Fertilizers offering the shareholders of the latter shares in Tata Chemicals in exchange.

It is always wise to be aware of preferential allotments being made and it can be very worthwhile to take these up when they come. Substantial profits can very often be made.

Rights Offers

A rights offer is on where existing shareholders are offered shares in the company as a "right" at a price below its market price. Thus, for example, in 2015 several companies issued rights shares the notable ones being Vascon Engineering, Tata Motors, GMR Infra, Zee Media, MIRC Electronics and Tata Power.

Although after the rights shares are issued the share will fall slightly in value, the investor still stands to make handsome gains.

Rights issues are made when a company is in need of capital which may be needed for:

1. Expansion programs; or
2. Diversification needs; or

3. Modernization of plant and machinery; or
4. Finance working capital, etc.

The shareholder is offered rights in proportion to his or her holding with a right to apply for more — the additional amount applied for is given only if there has not been great demand or if the issue has been over subscribed only nominally.

There are a few points to remember about rights issues. These include:

1. As the rights issue is offered at a price well and truly below the market price — you stand to make a good and quick gain.
2. The shareholder or investor is assured of a firm allotment.
3. The individual can if he so wishes sell his rights entitlement to another who may wish to purchase the shares. It is usually more profitable, however, to take up the rights and then sell the shares after the allotment of shares.

Apart from the above obvious benefits, rights appeal to shareholders for the following reasons also:

- These issues enable shareholders to increase their shareholding without diluting proportionate ownership in the company.
- Rights issues increase the dividend yield and improve the price earnings on the shares as they are usually below the market price of the shares.
- These issues enable shareholders to make additional investments in the company at an attractive price.

It is always wise to apply for more than one's right entitlement as rights are by and large not particularly popular and there is always the possibility of additional shares being allotted. Similarly, if one can get the rights entitlement of others, it is always worthwhile taking them up and make substantial gains.

In a nutshell, the rights offers are extremely worthwhile and should always be considered.

Private Placement

These occur when companies place a large amount of shares with another company or individual at an agreed or negotiated price. This is sometimes higher than the market price as the purchaser would be buying a significant amount and may get some say in the affairs of the company by being given a seat on the board, etc.

Others

Shares are also acquired in the following ways:

- **Inheritance:** An individual may inherit shares from a parent or relative.
- **Gift:** A parent or relative may gift an individual shares.
- **Private Transaction:** One may purchase a share from a friend or acquaintance privately. There is no bar to this and is often done. It is more common when individuals are buying a large chunk of a company S from the entity holding a substantial or controlling interest.

~

Chapter 12

~

The Importance of Information

"No one should buy a stock without knowing as much as possible about the company that issues it."

— J. Paul Getty

Successful investors purchase stocks in companies only after subjecting the company — its financial statements and its performance — to a piercing scrutiny and analysis. They invest on being convinced of its strengths and its likelihood of growth and prosperity. This is possible only by gathering as much information as is available on the company.

Informed investing is not groping in the dark. It is not purchasing a share because the company's name is attractive. Rather, it is investing in a company whose performance and strengths have been evaluated and the investment is made in a reasonable belief that the company is good and the price of its share will rise.

The information that one should seek to be able to invest knowledgeably can be broken down into:

- Information on the company — its performance, its sales, its profits and its products.
- Information on the company's performance in relation to other similar companies.
- Information on the industry in which the company operates. Industries go through periods of boom and depression. Some companies are more susceptible to economic depressions than others. It

is important to know at what stage of the economic cycle the company is in.

- Information on the economy. At a period of drought, agro-based industries would not do well.
- Information on government policy on legislation likely to be passed, on taxation to be imposed, or duties to be levied or reduced. All these would affect the performance of the company and as a result the share price.
- Information on consumer outlook and fashions and spending. These can be of prime importance.

In short, there is no such thing as irrelevant information. All information is useful. One must sift through it and determine how it would affect the company one is interested in and then act — either by purchasing, selling or holding its shares.

The usual sources of available information include:

1. The media;
2. Insiders;
3. Stock brokers;
4. Tips from colleagues, friends and acquaintances;
5. Professional investment consultants;
6. The internet; and
7. The annual report.

Media

The investing public is fortunate that there is today a multiplicity of magazines, periodicals and newspapers that focus their articles predominantly on companies and it is important that these be read and digested so that the decisions to buy, sell or hold are based on information and not on a reliable whim.

Newspapers

- The Economic Times;
- The Financial Express;
- The Business Standard;
- Business Line; and
- Mint.

Magazines

- Business India;
- Business World;
- Business Today; and
- Forbes India.

Television

- CNBC India;
- NDTV Profit;
- ET Now; and
- Business News Network.

The question that immediately arises is what kind of articles one could expect in these publications.

The newspapers inform one of the new issues that are open and about to open, the movement of shares over a period and during the preceding day and they often have a weekly pullout on companies and shares. They often publish information about the current performance of companies.

The business magazines are heavier reading. Their standard is high and they contain in-depth analysis of various industries and of companies. They discuss and they analyze in detail the performance of the companies and compare them with other similar ones thereby giving a reader a good perspective. They also contain knowledgeable articles on tax, investment strategies, finance and other allied subjects.

On television there are debates on company performance. Queries are answered and views are expressed. In addition, market prices are exhibited. This gives one a clear understanding of the state of the market and of particular companies.

It would be difficult and extremely time consuming to read all the publications mentioned. It can also be confusing. The investor should as a rule attempt to read one of the financial papers mentioned and at least two of the magazines. This would keep him reasonably well informed.

Insiders

Insiders are persons who work for a company or who have intimate dealings with a company and have access to or are aware of information that is not generally known (information in the public domain). This could be news of:

- Current performance;
- Announcement of a generous bonus issue;
- Large losses; and
- Other information that may impact stock prices.

Insiders are persons who are aware of news not available in the public domain that would shortly cause the price of the share to soar or fall. If one acts on insider information and purchases or sells shares (depending on the news), one can make a fortune and this is often done.

However, I caution all investors, in spite of the temptation, not to buy or sell based on insider information as it is illegal.

Stock Brokers

Stock brokers are a valuable source of information as they are in touch with the performance of companies, and news on the economy and the industry at all times. And most investors do seek their advice and base their decisions on investments on the suggestions made by their brokers.

A few words of warning, though:

- Stock brokers usually tend to look at companies from a very short term point of view — they rarely attempt to suggest or advise on how a company is likely to perform in two or three years in the future.
- A lot of information that a stock-broker may give is based on rumours and tips — many which may be untrue and unsubstantiated.
- The stock broker is very busy buying and selling umpteen shares. He rarely has the time to stand back and evaluate. As a result his advice is often not one that has been arrived at after deep reflection and thought.

- A stock broker could have vested interests. He may wish to get sell 1,000 shares of Pencils Ltd. In order to do so he may advise you to purchase it. The stock broker gains because he earns commission from both the seller and from you the purchaser. In short, it is in his interest to make you buy or to sell. He makes his commission.
- The stock broker's advice is usually based on "hot-tips" that he receives. X company is about to announce a bonus issue. X company is doing badly. By the time the news reaches the broker and then you — the market is most likely to have already reacted and so the news is not often going to be of much value.

This does not mean that one should not seek the views and advice of a stock broker. One must as it is such a valuable source of information. However, what one should not do is not to take it at its face value. Ponder on it, digest it and then relate it to information on the company received from other sources. If they agree and it feels right then act on it and you would usually be right.

Tips from Colleagues, Friends and Acquaintances

We Indians as a race are a people who talk too much — people love to gossip, to criticize, to spread rumours and to give advice and suggestions, very often unwelcome and unsought.

Everyone knows a sure bet — a company that is going places — a share that is going to double in three months. And your friends and colleagues will tell you about it. Listen to them. Listen, but then think. Research the company and if you think it makes sense invest or divest as the occasion calls for. Do not act unless you have checked it out through.

A person I know spoke to me about XYZ Ltd. He said that a friend of his had told him that the price was sure to rise. This was in August and the price was ₹ 19 per shares. The arguments and reasons he gave made sense and so my acquaintance purchased 1,000 shares. The price rose to ₹ 45. My acquaintance was able to sell his shares at ₹ 39 in October — an excellent profit in two months.

There is an interesting story on tips and rumours. Everyone gives them. There is a story of Joseph P. Kennedy, the father of President John Kennedy who amassed a fortune of over $ 250 million. This was largely from investments. In 1929 he was pondering on which share to buy. He spoke to his many influential friends; to the heads of large professional brokerage companies; to captains of industry and commerce. Each one gave him advice. Their opinions were often contradictory to one another leaving him confused. The opinions of four people that he respected was that the market was definitely going to rise. Pondering this he was walking down Wall Street when he came across a shoe-shine boy reading the *Wall Street Journal.* Out of curiosity he asked him his opinion. Promptly the boy said "Buy oils and rails. The price is booming." Whereupon Joe Kennedy walked away from Wall Street having decided that a market so rampant with tips and predictions was not for him especially at such a tumultuous time. His logic was that if a shoe-shine boy was giving hot tips, then the market was possibly overpriced and it was a good time to cash out. He wasn't wrong. The market crashed later that year and what happened then is history.

Bernard Baruch, the legendary figure of Wall Street who began his career as a messenger boy and became a multimillionaire and adviser to U.S. presidents, went to a barber at Wall Street every day. This was not to get a haircut or a shave but to listen in to conversations between market men and to hear from his barber Tony what had been discussed earlier that day. Acting on such information, and after verifying it for himself, he made a fortune.

Professional Investment Consultants

The last two decades has seen the growth of a multiplicity of professional investment consultants. They offer advice on which shares should be purchased, held or sold. They manage portfolios and recommand investment that should be made.

These consultants are expensive. They usually charge a fee which is around five per cent of the market value of the investments that one wishes to make. For a similar fee they would manage your portfolio too. They often specify a minimum value for your portfolio. Such services are usually beyond the reach of the small investor.

Many of these consultants bring out weekly or monthly news letters. These vary enormously in content and quality. Some rely heavily on charts and technical analysis whereas others are more future oriented. Most of them are extremely useful. Many however are shoddy and extremely badly researched. Prior to actually acting on them, you must think carefully.

Internet

On the Internet there are portals that have a tremendous amount of information on companies and the manner shares have moved. These include sharekhan.com, moneycontrol.com and the websites of the Bombay Stock Exchange and the National Stock Exchange.

Company Annual Reports

The annual report of companies gives one the most detailed information about the performance of a company and the information that it gives must be carefully analyzed and digested.

~

Chapter 13

~

The Importance of a Company's Management

Prior to purchasing the shares of a company it is imperative to assess the quality, competence and integrity of the management as it is upon them that the future of the company rests. A good, innovative management can make a company grow and a bad one can kill it. Chrysler, in the United States, was an ailing giant. Iacocca, with shrewd policies and tight, tough management made it profitable once more. In the mid 1990s, Apple was on the brink of bankruptcy after Jobs' ouster. After bringing him back the fortunes changed and because most valuable company in history. Other turnarounds include IBM under Lou Gerstner and Fedex by Fred Smith.

Nearer home, Kingfisher and United Breweries bit the dust due to the persons at the helm. As did Satyam. The failures of blue chips such as Metal Box and Killick Nixon can be attributed to decisions made by the management. On the other hand, others have grown on account of the foresight and drive of their management — Tata under Ratan Tata, Infosys under its founders, Wipro under Azim Premji, Kotak Mahindra under Uday Kotak and Mahindra & Mahindra first under Keshub and then Anand Mahindra.

What is evident in this is that it is recognized that the man or group at the helm can determine the fortunes of a company and it is for this reason that one should not invest in shares of any company until the quality of its management has been assessed.

In India, management can be broadly divided into two types:

- Family management.
- Professional management.

Family Management

The seats of power in family managed companies are occupied by the members of a family and the mantle of leadership and control over the affairs of the company are passed down from father to sons or from brother to brother or cousin to cousin. This is a phenomenon pronounced in India and many of the larger Indian companies are family controlled — prominent examples being the Birlas, the Tatas, the Ambanis, the Goenkas, and the Singhanias.

In most family managed companies, the management often runs the company as its very own. Decisions are made with family interests in view. Cash-rich companies are used to buy other companies with scant regard to income distribution to share holders. Chabbria's use of cash-rich Dunlop and Goenka's use of Ceat funds for acquisitions are prime examples of this. Employees, including senior managers, are considered paid employees of the family and are, unfortunately at times, treated as such. I remember an incident that happened a few years ago which has cast an indelible mark in my mind. It was at Mumbai airport. The head of a large business house was going abroad. The chief executives of his companies were around him — men famous in their fields, respected and competent. When their leader was about to go through immigration these captains of industry (some much older than their master) bent double and touched their leader's feet as a sign of respect or subservience (I know not which) and their heads were touched as a sign of blessing by their master with a smile. I dread to think what would have happened to the career of one of these managers had he not touched his chairman's feet. In short, employees in family managed companies are expected to be subservient to the family and family loyalty is often the most important attribute required for an employee. I know that in a prominent company controlled by a very famous Marwari family all family members are addressed as "babu." Loyalty to the family is rewarded too. If a retainer is ill he is looked after and when he retires he is given a good pension. A loyal executive of a very large family managed company in Kolkata died a premature death. The company gave his wife a job and educated his children. I know of no multinational that would do this.

The other concern I have is with regard to company assets. Who uses the company assets and for what? I remember meeting a member of a prominent business family at a function a couple of years ago. He mentioned that he could not stay late as he had a flight at 6.00 A.M. to Europe. I naturally wished him an enjoyable holidays. He interjected that he has a Board Meeting in Malaga during this week. He was, with five others of his immediate family, flying in the company jet to Turkey, then to Italy and then to Malaga and would be returning after going to England. Who was paying for this? The service tax department seized for auctioning in December 2015 a plane purchased at $ 22 million used by Mr. Vijay Mallya and which was purportedly embellished with paintings by Piccasso and other masters. Was this from Company funds? Were the shareholders aware? These are questions that must arise when one looks at companies controlled by one individual or by a family.

Many family controlled companies are rigid, orthodox and traditional. This has been mainly on account of family businesses being managed at the helm by patriarchs who have not been exposed to the modern methods of management. This is changing now. The scions of the large business houses have gone abroad. Many like Anand Mahindra and Anil Ambani have been educated at prestigious business schools and have been managing their business. The old guard changeth. Modern methods of management are being used effectively and the businesses are thriving. Yet in spite of all this in family managed businesses it is the family that matters and it is the family that decides on what course of action should be taken, what should be done and who should be at the helm. The chief executive will always be a family member.

Professional Management

Professionally managed companies are those that are managed by employees — by those who do not usually have a financial stake in the company and have been chosen to manage the affairs of the company on account of their proven competence and expertise.

Professional managers depend on success in achieving laid down goals and results to retain their positions. They are constantly set targets of growth to achieve. Consequently they tend to be efficient, cost effective, cost conscious and stable. There is usually a method in the way the business is managed and there is reasoning and logic in their decisions. As they are accountable, they tend to be careful and conscientious.

Professional managers are prepared to listen to new ideas and try out new products. They are receptive and seek to ensure their methods are the best. They try to be aware of the latest break-throughs in science, technology, electronics and management science. Consequently professionally managed companies are normally well organized, growth oriented and good performers. Investors are the recipients of regular dividends and bonus issues. This is good.

However, there is, in professionally managed companies, a lot of infighting and internal politics. Managers are, as their promotions, etc. are dependent on performance, always trying to outshine one another. This does not happen usually in family controlled companies as all are aware that the mantle of power will always be on the shoulders of a family member.

What then are the things one should look at when considering investing in a company?

1. In my opinion the most important aspect is proven competence — the management's past record. How has the company been managed in the previous three to five years? Has the growth been impressive or lacklustre?
2. How high is the regard or esteem in which the management is held by its peers in the business community and in the industry?
3. The depth of knowledge of the management too must be considered, including their knowledge of the industry and of the latest innovations and management techniques.
4. How did the management manage at a time of adversity? Anyone can make profits in a boom. The acid test is how a management performs at a time of adversity? Did the company perform better than its competitors?
5. The management's integrity must be beyond question.
6. The management must be innovative. A management that does not look to the future and plan its strategy for the future is not likely to grow at the same pace as its competitors.

Prior to Investing

1. It would be wise to think thrice before one invests in a company that has yet to professionalize its management. This is especially true regarding family run companies as the direction of the company's growth would be based on the wishes of the family which may not be in the best interests of the company. Decisions taken may be arrived at considering the good of the family. There may be nepotism with family members occupying positions of power on account of blood and not competence.
2. It is important to determine who the major shareholders are and ascertain whether they have a record of managing share prices, especially at times when they are trying to raise money from the general public through share issues and debentures.
3. It would be wise to avoid investing in companies where there is infighting or where promoter families have split as the one who suffers most is the small shareholder.
4. It is prudent to avoid investing in the shares of an unknown business house.
5. Finally, one should avoid investing in companies where the management is no longer dynamic.

In India, apart from some multi-nationals, the larger companies are family owned. However, their saving grace is that although at the helm they are dominated by a member of the family the companies are managed on a day to day basis by professional managers. Additionally, the scions of families are increasingly enlightened and knowledgeable, often having been educated at prestigious business schools. A family that is managing three companies well is more than likely to be managing the fourth well also.

The bottom line in determining the competence or incompetence of the management is naturally "the bottom line." How much has it grown? This is the real test and one should not invest in a company in which one has doubts on the competence or integrity of its management.

~

Chapter 14

~

Investing on Hot Tips

Man is avaricious by nature. He is hungry for tips that he can use for his profit. And as a race, we love to give tips. Nowhere is the giving and the quest for tips more frequent than among individuals active in the stock market. The tippers are at their enthusiastic best when the markets are on an upward swing, They would call you and whisper, “XYZ will hit ₹ 120 a share. Buy ABC. MNO will double in 2 months; RSP will soar to ₹ 300,” and the likes. Most of those giving the tips were well intentioned people who had genuinely hope that their friend would make a lot of money. They may also have invested in the share. And this is how many shares are bought. This is to a great extent because the average investor is normally a little confused with the large number of shares that are available for purchase. He may not have access to information on how companies are doing. In fact he often does not know what certain companies actually do. He has money which he wishes to invest but is uncertain on which share to buy. If at this stage a banker friend or a broker or even a knowledgeable friend rings him and whispers conspiratorially “Trichur Chemicals is going to be taken over by Continental Pearls and the price will rise from its present price of ₹ 12 to ₹ 50 at the least,” the individual would be incredibly restrained if he says, “Thanks, but no, I am not interested.” What he will do is, depending on his liquidity, buy some shares. Then being altruistic or a big talker (or both) he will mention this to a friend, embellishing the details a little. This would go on until many people get this information and act. There is also another source of tips — newspapers and magazines. On reading these tips a lot of people purchase the shares and because of all this activity prices may rise momentarily — and then they fall. This is because the activity has resulted in the price rising to a level that often cannot be sustained. This may not necessarily happen but to be safe one should remember the following:

- Often large investors spread rumours when they wish to off-load a large block of shares and do not wish the price to fall (as it would do) if supply is greater than demand. By creating an artificial interest they are able to successfully sell their holding at a profit. Several financial papers and magazines and some investment advisers have been accused of recommending investments which they wish to sell. As their opinions are respected, individuals buy to their detriment.
- It is not prudent to buy on the basis of public tips, such as recommendations in the newspapers or magazines. This is because by the time the magazine or newspaper is printed, published and in your hands, the information would be stale. Additionally many others who have received the "tip" before you may have purchased the share. The result is if one buys the shares it would at a high price.
- It is difficult to distinguish between a genuine tip and another. When in doubt, don't. It is usually not worth it.
- There are genuine tips. A manager or a director of a company may tell you in confidence that the company's exports have increased by 40 per cent or that the company is going to probably consider the declaration of a bonus in a few months. However, this is insider information and should not be acted on as it is illegal.

In some instances the tip or information is given well before attention is focused on the company or the public is aware of its performance or results. If you are fortunate enough to get information of this nature, you should act immediately. Delay would be unwise. At a party in December 2014 a very senior finance official in ABC Ltd. mentioned to a friend of mine that the ABC Ltd. has turned the corner and that it may be worth his while to purchase some shares in the company. At that time the shares were traded at ₹ 19 a share. He did not act. In six months the price soared to nearly ₹ 80 a share and stabilized at around ₹ 100 a share. He has always regretted it. Similarly, in July 2014 a colleague began talking to a person who during the conversation told him that he was working as the personnel manager of a large company. He was bemoaning the fact that two of their factories were about to be locked out on account of a union dispute. As soon as he could, this colleague, sold his shares in the company. Two days later a newspaper report published the fact that the factories had been locked out. The shares plunged. My colleague saved himself from worry and a loss by acting decisively and speedily.

When one does receive a tip the things to do are:

1. Check how long it has been a "hot tip." If everyone has been talking about it for some time it is no longer a worthwhile tip and it is best to ignore it. It would already be a high price. One must act on a tip when it is "hot," not when it is known to ten thousand others.
2. Check on the reliability of the tip. "Hot tips" are dime, a dozen and everyone but everyone and his brother have a few hot tips. Ninety nine percent of these are probably only wishful thinking. It would be wise to consider the following :

   - How reliable is the person who has given the tip?
   - What has one's past experience been with this source?
   - What is the "source of the tip"? Has the informant got the information from someone knowledgeable?
   - How many others are privy to the tip?
   - How old is the tip?
   - Has the informant himself acted on the information and either bought or sold shares?

On receiving a tip it is also important to consider the company. What is the general working of the company, its size, its managements, its range of products and its performance?

It is imprudent to invest until one gets all the details one needs regarding the reasons for the likely rise or fall in the share and investigate it. As soon as a tip is received do not rush in. It could be to your financial loss.

A huge word of caution though. You should also check on who has given you the tip. If it is a person who has information on the company and is in possession of information that is not in the public domain, and you act on this information, you'd be guilty of insider trading which is an offence.

~

Chapter 15

~

Spotting Market Leaders

One makes money on the stock exchange not by following the crowd, but by spotting budding market leaders at an early stage and then betting on them.

A colleague of mine was renovating his house and his contractor suggested that he tile his house with a certain brand. These tiles had been introduced only a little while earlier. He liked it and used it. During the next few months, he came across many establishments (hotels, houses and offices) that had the same tiles. Believing that this company had a good product and a good future, he bought shares in the company. He has never regretted it and has seen his original investment appreciate several times. He was lucky and shrewd to identify a budding market leader. This was by chance. There are other ways one can identify them.

Great Product

A company's sales and its profitability ultimately depend on its product — its quality, price and acceptability in the market place. A new company with a good, superior product has the potential of becoming a leader.

Superior Performance

It is important to examine a company's performance (growth in sales, profits, etc.) with other companies in the industry. If the company is consistently bettering the industry average, it is a company that may be worthy of investing in.

Capable and Honest Management

No investment must be made without critically examining the competence and reputation of the management. The management, by its policies, controls the destiny of a company. While a superior management can make it grow; a timid, incompetent management can ruin the company.

Monopoly

In some industries, certain companies enjoy a virtual monopoly. These are good companies to invest in.

Cyclicality

Certain industries are cyclical and its fortunes fluctuate. This especially happens with great periodicity in the textile and shipping industries.

~

Chapter 16

~

Evaluating Industry Risks

Apart from examining the financial strengths of a company, a potential investor or lender must examine the industry within which the company operates because this could affect the very survival of the company. A company's management may be superior, its balance sheet strong and its reputation enviable. However, the company may not have diversified and the industry within which it operates may be at a depression. This could result in a tremendous decline in revenues which could threaten the very continuance of the company.

Many business magazines carry detailed industry analyses as do financial newspapers. It would be wise to read and compare the various analyses as it would give one an indication regarding the industry. If the industry is forecasted to boom, it would be a worthwhile proposition to invest in the company as the likelihood of rewards are great. Conversely, if the industry is projected to take a downturn, the wise man would quickly divert his investment.

What are the factors one should consider when one examines the industry within which a company operates?

Is It Easy to Enter the Industry?

An easy entry industry requires little capital. It does not require much technological expertise either. As a consequence there are a multitude of competitors. This could result eventually in intense competition resulting in very low margins and high costs.

Are there Many Competitors?

If there are many and no single competitor dominates, then each of the competitors will vie with each other for a greater market share. There will be price wars and margins will reduce. A striking example of this is the TV market where there are many companies. Similarly there are many companies selling personal computers. Each company is trying to outdo the other and to do so are offering more to the consumer for less.

Is the Company in a High Growth Industry?

If the growth of the industry is over 30% p.a., new players and companies are attracted to it, in the hope of earning super profits. This leads to greater competition. The major high growth industries presently are several — Information Technology, E-Commerce, Telecom, Healthcare, Retail, Transportation, Education and Training and Banking and Insurance. Some which were earlier high growth such as real estate, manufacturing, etc. are no longer growing as they did earlier.

Is there Product Differentiation?

A company whose products have product differentiation has more staying power. The products of a company may be preferred because of its name or because of the quality of its products — Mercedes Benz cars or Iphones or Levis jeans or Samsung refrigerators or Sumeet food processors. People are prepared to pay more for the product and consequently the products are at premium and above competition.

Does the Company have a High Fixed Cost Structure?

If it does it would have large investments and a large capital base and because of this it will not have too many competitors. Its high fixed costs would have to be serviced and a fall in sale can result in a more than proportionate fall in profits. An example of such an industry is the auto industry, which requires enormous capital investment. The number of companies in this industry is a few and they cater to specific segments of the population.

What is the Cost of Capacity Additions?

If the cost of expansion is high, competitors will be few. Consequently, there will also be greater economies of scale.

What is the Size of Exit Costs?

If the costs of exit are great, i.e. the payment of gratuity, unfunded provident and pension liabilities and the likes — companies would remain in the business even if the margins are low and little or no profits are being made.

What is the Motivation of Competitors?

Are they in the market for prestige or for profit? If profit is not the motivating factor, companies may remain in the industry even at slender margins.

Is there a Substitute Product?

Can another product replace the product? The industry where this is constantly looked at is the packaging industry — beer cans replacing bottles, PVC replacing conventional paper wrapping, jute bags replacing plastic bags and so on. The list is endless.

How Powerful are the Buyers and the Suppliers?

If they are powerful they can force prices down or up which could be to the detriment of the industry. In scarce economies such as India, it is often the suppliers of raw materials who wield enormous power. They dictate terms, insist on payment upfront and keep to their own schedules.

What will be the Effect of Technological Innovations on the Product?

Would it result in it becoming obsolete? An industry where great strides in technology have been made in recent years is the computer industry — with its omnis, personal computers, laptops and now it is the palmtops and PDAs. The things they are capable of are phenomenal and the question being asked is — what next?

Is there Great Rivalry between Existing Competitors?

Such as price competition and advertising wars. This can erode profits. In India, presently there is fierce competition in the electronic sector. If there is heavy advertising and large discounts being given, margins get eroded. This naturally leads to lower profits.

What is the Impact of Government Policy?

This can attract or detract competitors. It can also result in higher or lower profits. This is why industry waits anxiously every February for the budget because it is this that will largely determine the company's results in the next year. However, with liberalization this is not as critical as it was before but it can affect, especially if new taxes are imposed or new duties levied.

Are there International Cartels?

In the coffee industry, the supply far exceeds the demand. In order to protect against widely fluctuating prices, the International Coffee Organization which is made up of coffee exporting and importing countries have fixed the price of a bag of coffee and the quantity that a company may export. In such situations a coffee exporting company is assured of a sale, a definite price and certain profit.

While examining and studying the industry in which a company operates it is important to also study demand for the products of the industry and of the company in particular. The items one should consider when assessing demand are:

- Is the business in a high growth industry and if so, can management operate at a high level? Low growth can be alright as the business may be able then to finance its activity with internally generated funds.
- How essential is the product or is it just a fad?
- Is the demand predictable? In the food industry demand is predictable whereas it is not so in the refrigerator industry.
- Is the business volatile? For example, financed businesses are usually very volatile.
- Is the demand cyclical? Demand may be only periodic.
- What would happen to the product demand if a structural change takes place in the economy? For example, in 1973 the OPEC cartel affected many industries.
- What would be the effect on demand if a change in government policy takes place? A high tax on imports can stimulate demand

for domestic products. Similarly if the government reduces import duty on certain articles, demand can shift to imported items.

- How will exchange fluctuations affect demand? In 1984, for example, the pound strengthened and this cut the costs of imports into the United Kingdom and stimulated consumer demand. Similarly, a weakening of the rupee makes Indian articles more cost attractive abroad.

Another factor which is important is that all industries have cycles. The initial period is known as the sunrise. This is a period of growth and their growth is usually quite remarkable. It apexes at noon. At this time there are many competitors and the industry is maturing. Up to this period, it is good to enter the industry as the profits make it more than worthwhile. Then comes a period of consolidation which last for some time. Eventually demand falls, noon becomes evening then dusk, and finally sunset. Investing in a sunset industry is short-sighted as the investment is likely to turn sour.

In brief, it is imperative that at the time a company is being considered for investment, that the industry the company is operating in is considered as this will determine whether the investment will be profitable or not.

~

Chapter 17

~

Country Analysis

Cross country exposure is the amount of money lent or invested in another country. The exposure that the entity has is that if that country goes through an economic downturn, suffer a revolution or turmoil, the money lent or invested can be at risk. 2014 and 2015 has been classic years. The Greek Government went bankrupt and nearly left the Euro, there has been conflict in the Middle East, Syria on account of ISIS is in turmoil, etc. Monies lent / invested in these countries are at risk — one may either not get it back or the value may, because of inflation be eroded. Earlier many American banks suffered enormous losses in Latin American loans. The reason has been that the countries in Latin America were unable to repay the loans they had taken. A similar problem existed in Africa too — in countries like Nigeria that had severe balance of payments problems.

The message is clear. Whenever a person is examining the annual report of a company he should also study the country in which it operates — whether it is dependent on another country for its imports or exports and the stability of that other country. The areas that should be considered are:

1. The Political Stability of the Country

The political stability of a country is of paramount importance. No industry or company can survive or grow in a country in political turmoil. In disturbed times there is great uncertainty. Survival is a day to day affair and dependent not on industry but on the benevolence of those in power. A company could prosper one day and be in the doldrums in the next. A recent example that comes to mind is Sri Lanka — a beautiful island which was thriving as an exporter of tea, a tourist's paradise and a producer of pearls and precious stones. This country then plunged into a civil war and the economy became a mess. No industry or company can thrive in such an environment.

2. The Rate of Inflation

Inflation has an enormous affect. If the rate of inflation in the country from which one imports is high, then the cost of production will automatically go up. This might reduce the cost competitiveness of the product finally manufactured. Conversely if the rate of inflation in the country to which one exports is high, the products manufactured would become more attractive resulting in increased sales. Some countries such as South Sudan and Venezuela have inflation of 73.60% and 68.50% respectively. Money had no real value. However, exports from these countries were attractive purely because on account of their galloping inflation and consequent devaluation of their currency, their products were cheaper than those of others. Advanced countries such as the United States and the United Kingdom have at 0.50% and 0.10% very little inflation.

3. Foreign Exchange Risk

This is real risk and one must be cognizant of the effect of a revaluation or devaluation of the currency either in the home country or in the country the company deals in. Devaluation in the home country would make the products the company makes more attractive in other countries. It would also make imports more expensive which could have an adverse effect on sales. Devaluation in the country to which the company exports would make the company's products more expensive. To hedge against devaluation in the country from which one imports, most companies enter into a forward foreign exchange contract thereby crystalising the amount of the liability and ensuring that the company would not be exposed to an unexpected loss should a devaluation occur.

4. Nationalization

This is a real threat in many countries — the fear that a company may become nationalized. Historically (with very few exceptions), nationalized companies are less efficient than their private sector counterparts. If one is dependent on a company for certain supplies, nationalization could result in supplies become erratic and the likes.

5. Restrictive Practices

Restrictive practices or cartels imposed by countries can affect, depending on the companies needs, its imports or exports. The USA has restrictions regarding the imports of a variety of articles like textiles, etc. Licenses are given and amounts that may be imported from companies or countries are clearly detailed. India has a number of restrictions on what may be imported and at what rate of duty. This, to an extent, determines the prices at which the goods can be sold. If the domestic industry is to be supported, the duties levied may be increased resulting in imports becoming unattractive.

It is, therefore, important when viewing a company to see how sensitive it is to governmental policies and the extent changes can affect the company.

6. Economic / Business Cycle

Economic / business cycle in a country can drastically affect the performance of a company. During a period of recession, demand is low and sales are low. Companies at this time often suffer a large fall in profits and even losses. Conversely at a period of recovery or boom consumer demand is high, sales are on the increase and so are profits.

While analyzing a company operating in another country one should determine:

- The stage of the economic / business cycle.
- The expected duration of the cycle.
- The company's ability to survive as demonstrated previously to weather recession.
- At what stage of the cycle the company is likely to be most affected.

It is important to remember that losses are always at a time when accelerating inflation is followed by recession. There is, however, nothing to suggest that a boom or a recession would be for a definite period of time and hence the length of previous cycles should not be used as a measure to forecast the length of an existing cycle.

~

Chapter 18
~
The Best Time to Buy Shares

"You don't buy a stock because it has real value. You buy it because you feel there is always a greater fool down the street ready to pay more than you paid."
— Donald S. Stocking, U.S. Securities & Exchange Commission

Mr. Stocking notwithstanding, the whole investment decision — on whether one does well or not so well in regard to an investment is based on one criteria — when should the share be bought? After having identified the share to buy it is important to decide when and at what price. It is on these two that the result lies.

Prices of shares fluctuate daily for a diverse number of reasons — the breath of scandal in high place, the threat of war, drought, floods, etc. Also, prices can fluctuate widely.

In November 2015, for example, the shares of Dr. Reddy fell by 11.6% on news of its manufacturing facilities at Srikakulam and oncology formulation facility at Duvvada in Andhra Pradesh getting a warning letter from US FDA. The price fell despite the company stating that there was nothing wrong with its facilities. Later in December, when this was confirmed the prices began to inch up.

It is not very difficult to choose the shares to purchase. There is a host of information available on companies to assist one in choosing a share. However, prices fluctuate daily and no one can say whether the prices will fall or rise, next and, by how much, unless he is blessed with the gift of Nostradamas. So the question arises — at what price should the shares be bought?

There is no fool-proof method or any guarantee that the price chosen would be the lowest but the following rules will ensure that the price at which the shares are bought will not be ridiculously high:

1. It is very important that a share be not bought at a time when the prices have risen sharply because historically and logically the price will fall as sharply. This is so as the demand / popularity is likely to fall.
2. It is not very wise to purchase a share that everyone is talking about — a share that is felt to be a "sure winner." This is so because "everyone" is likely to be buying share that resulting in its price being artificially high. Demand will usually be higher than supply. In due course, the public will lose interest in the share. Then the price will fall. That would be the time to purchase it.
3. Sometimes the price of a share may register a fall for no real reason apart from a general gloom in the market. This is usually a good time to buy. In 2015, on account of various world events and because India's economy had not grown as anticipated, the Sensex fell by 25%. There were many companies doing very well and it was clearly a time to purchase good shares at low prices.
4. It is dangerous to purchase shares when the prices of all shares in the industry / market are falling as it would be uncertain how much the shares would fall. One should wait and watch and only purchase when the prices stabilize.
5. The earlier highs and lows of shares must be studied in depth for a feel of the company. And at the time of purchasing a share it is always useful to remember the following rules:

   - Purchase a share as close to its lowest price in the previous year.
   - Never buy a share in normal circumstances at a price higher than its highest price in the previous year. However, this does not hold good in a boom period when the prices are rising with enormous rapidity. At such times one may purchase shares at around its highest price in the previous year.
   - A share should be purchased at a price that is between the lowest price of the previous and the average price for the year.

- One should try not to purchase a share which is significantly higher than its average price of the previous year.

6. The best time to purchase a share, which you feel is going to do well, is much before its results are likely to be out — possibly two or three months after its Annual General Meeting when people have forgotten about its previous years results and are now looking at other companies.
7. Shares of companies that are creating an awareness of their presence in the market are good shares to buy.
8. The price of shares goes up just when a company begins, or announces, its commercial production, or when a new project goes on stream. A purchaser, anticipating this, should always buy a share just before commercial production starts — at a time when the price is a little depressed. This depression reflects the caution of the market — will the project be viable? Will the production actually start?
9. Shares of companies rise on the announcement of good news. Purchase of shares on the day the news is announced is usually safe as depending on the news the price will rise on the next and subsequent days. Better still is to purchase on the anticipation of good news.
10. Companies frequently give reports on their performance. Indian stock exchanges have now made it mandatory that all listed companies announce their quarterly results. These along with its note on activities if they are favourable push the price up. One should try and purchase the share the day the report appears because otherwise the price will rise too high. This point must be taken with some caution. If the price has risen in anticipation of stunning news and the results are not stunning, the price will fall.
11. It is important to keep an eye on the operating results of other companies in the same industry. If other companies in the industry are doing well, it is likely that the company in question will also do well. On the other hand, if all others are doing badly so would the company whose shares are being considered.

Chapter 19

~

The Right Time to Sell

Selling is infinitely more difficult than buying. If a share is falling in price one does not want to sell and suffer a loss. On the other hand, when a share is rising in price one does not want to sell as one's greed leads one to believe that it will go higher and higher. And of course there are emotional attachments — one wishes to hold and to cherish the first share one bought or the share received as a gift on one's twenty-first birthday.

The sceptic would initially query — why sell? Why not hold on forever. But this is not always possible. So what then are the reasons to sell?

The Reasons for Selling

There are several:

1. If a share is falling in price rapidly and unlikely to rise again it is wise to sell and cut your losses — even if it means admitting that you were wrong in the choice of your share. A person I know bought shares in a company at ₹ 36 per share. The price began to fall rapidly. As he did not want to book a loss he held on. Six years later when he wished to sell the shares there were no takers anywhere. This may be an extreme example but is true.
2. Selling is useful if you feel you were wrong in purchasing a particular share for whatever the reason — it is in the wrong industry — it is not a growth share — whatever. Selling will help to get rid of the shares from your portfolio.

3. It is important to regularly (say quarterly or if you have the time — monthly) go through your portfolio and see how well the shares have done and whether they have done as well as you had anticipated. If some have not and are unlikely to do so, it is best to sell them and buy new shares that have better prospects. This is known as "weeding."
4. Selling shares when the price has for some reason zoomed gives you an opportunity to take advantage of the upswing and should be used whenever possible. If later you wish to repurchase the shares again one can do so when the price falls and stabilizes.
5. Shares need to be sold too in situations when liquid cash is required — for marriage, repay loans, purchase a house or to pay for some major expense.

The Right Price to Sell

The next question that will inevitably arise is that now that you have decided to sell, at what price and when should the share be sold?

1. As a general rule, as soon as you have made a profit of 20% on your investment, sell 25% of the shares that you purchased. Then when it appreciates a further 10%, sell another 25%. The balance can be held or sold after you feel the growth in price will stagnate (*see* Illustration 19.1).

Illustration 19.1

For example, in 2014 Ram bought 4,000 shares at ₹ 25 each of Comforters Ltd. The price rose to ₹ 30 by March 2015 at which time he sold 1,000 shares. In June 2015 the price had risen to 33 at which time he sold another 1,000 shares. In August 2015 the price was ₹ 38 per share when he sold another 25%.

	₹	₹
Purchase of 4,000 shares @ ₹ 25 per share		100,000
Sale Price March 2015 — 1,000 @ ₹ 30	30,000	
Sale Price June 2015 – 1,000 @ ₹ 33	33,000	
Sale Price August 2015 – 1,000 @ ₹ 38	38,000	101,000
Net Investment		(1,000)

On selectively selling his shares Ram has procured ₹ 1,01,000 on selling 3,000 shares a gain of ₹ 1,000 over his original investment. Furthermore, he still holds 1,000 shares.

2. In any case it is important to sell shares once a profit of over 75% has been achieved. This should be done even if you feel the share will rise further in price. It must be remembered that the price of a share that has gone up can also go down (*see* Illustration 19.2).

Illustration 19.2

In mid-20XX the price of ABC suddenly rose from ₹ 19 per share, within the space of a month to ₹ 45. Daniel had bought 500 shares at ₹ 30. Joseph too had bought 500 shares at ₹ 31. When the price reached 43 Joseph sold 300 shares. Daniel held on. Joseph sold a further 100 shares at 41. The price fell to 29 by October 20XX. The effects of their share dealing are as follows:

	₹
Daniel	
Purchased 500 shares @ ₹ 30 per share	15,000
Current price 500 shares @ ₹ 29 per share	14,500
Book Loss.	(500)
Joseph	
Purchased 500 shares @ ₹ 31 per share	15,500
Sold 300 shares @ ₹ 43 per share	(12,900)
Sold 100 shares @ ₹ 41 per share	(4,100)
Profit on 400 shares	
300 @ ₹ 12 per share	3,600
100@ ₹ 10 per share	1,000
	4,600

Daniel did not dispose of any share in the belief that the price would go up. Joseph on the other hand, sold most of his holdings, realized his original investment, booked an actual profit of ₹ 4,600 and still has 100 shares.

3. At the time of purchasing a share, one must decide at what price to sell the share at. This is important and this discipline must be kept. It is often hard especially when the price is rising but one must, at these times, realize that the price can also fall.
4. One should sell when the price begins to fall and is unlikely to rise in the foreseeable future. This is based on the principle of "cut your losses by taking a loss" because the earlier the loss is taken the better. It is pointless holding on to the share in the belief that the price will rise.

John bought 1,000 shares of a non banking finance company during its initial public offer at ₹ 52 per share in 2007. The company has been plagued with several issues and its shares have been quoting in 2015 at ₹ 5 per share — at 10% of its issue price and 50% of its face value. As the prices fell he held on in the belief that the price will go up. He still holds it. He has not earned on his investment either.

5. It's wise to sell shares immediately after a capital issue — especially one that has been oversubscribed by at least 5 or 6 times. In the euphoria of the public issue shares are often quoted at price much higher than its realistic price — the price to which it would sink to in a few months.
6. Always sell a share when the price has risen very sharply because the price can fall just as sharply.
7. Whenever there is a doubt in regard to a share — sell. This is very important. One must be sure and comfortable with one's portfolio. One must never feel he has 2 or 3 potential lemons in his portfolio.

   Roger had been becoming increasingly uneasy about his holdings of XYZ Ltd. as in his opinion the company was going through a traumatic period. If Roger was uneasy, he must sell his holdings irrespective of whether his feelings were justified or not.
8. It is impossible to ever determine the peak. Therefore, whenever the objective one has is reached and the profit required made — sell. The share may go up. It does not matter. The profit that was aimed at has been made.
9. It is also wise to sell when the price / earnings ratio is very high. At a high P/E ratio the company has to have a very high rate of growth. This is not often possible. As a thumb rule, one should consider selling once the price earnings (P/E) ratio is higher than 35.
10. It is important to remember that if all the prices are falling, then the shares should not be sold as the circumstances may be on account of certain other factors.
11. A share should not be sold if its price has fallen for no major reason as in all likelihood it will improve.

Chapter 20

~

Long Term Investment

One of the major reasons for the purchase of shares is to have a hedge against inflation. Equity shares are also purchased to build up the net worth of the individual, channelise savings and to build an alternate source of income. These are very valid reasons and the market prices of all major company shares have risen at a rate much higher than that of inflation. In India, the average long term compounded annual growth rate (CAGR) of the shares has been over 13% which is higher than that of any other investment. Indiviually, some shares have done even better. For example, if one had invested ₹ 1 lakh in Symphony Ltd. in 2005, in 2015 it would have been worth ₹ 26 lakh. That is a huge appreciation.

Such returns can be achieved only if shares are held for a period of time and not as short term investments. The shares must be held for some time for the fruits of the effort to be clear and visible. There are, however, important points that one must remember in the regard.

1. The shares should be bought in high growth companies. If the growth of the company is practically slow, then it is more than likely that the dividends would be small and the increase in market price practically non-existent. In a growth company, profits increase rapidly resulting in bonus shares and dividends and even a modest investment can grow into a handsome corpus. Sometimes even a fortune.

2. The investor should not expose himself to the vagaries of any single industry. If all the shares owned are in a single company, then should that industry go through a recession, the value of the investment would fall. Additionally, the investor will receive no income. The investor should, therefore, diversify his investment as much as possible — he should buy shares of good companies in different industries.
3. An investor must keep a watchful eye on all his investments and he must act quickly and decisively if a company is not performing as well as it was expected to.
4. The investor must also be aware of other high growth companies and industries and must be able to switch if necessary to other companies to assure himself of high returns and growth in the value of his investment. In choosing a company certain criteria should be looked for:
   - The company should be in a high growth industry.
   - It must be one of the leading companies in the concerned industry.
   - It must be well managed.
   - There must be demand and market acceptance for its products.
   - It must have a history of dividend payments and bonus issues.
   - Since the shares are purchased for long term investment, day to day price fluctuations may be ignored. What matters is that in a period of say, 2 or 3 years the share must fulfil the expectations placed on it.
   - If the price falls below the floor price decided by the investor he should purchase more as the gains would be much higher.

Should Shares Held As Long Term Investment Ever Be Sold?

The question that is rightly asked is whether shares purchased as long term investments should ever be sold.

The answer is that, yes, they must be sold under certain conditions:

1. A growth company in a growth industry can cease being a growth company in a growth industry. The boom may be over and it may be going through a recession. It is important to divest at such times.

2. Man is an imperfect creature. He is not infallible and is prone to making errors of judgement. The moment it is felt that a mistake had been made, the concerned share must be sold.
3. Sell to take advantage of tax exemptions — especially long term capital gains.
4. The investor should sell if the company is not doing as well as other companies in the same industry and switch investments to get the maximum return on his investment.
5. Consider selling if the price has shot up all of a sudden. This might be due to some unusual happening. If you like the share you can always buy it back when the price falls.

Advantages of Long Term Investment

The advantages of long term investment are money.

1. The investor saves on the payment of regular brokerage fees.
2. The investor, as he diversifies his portfolio, spreads his risks.
3. As long term investment focuses on which share to buy, at what price, and when, the shift of emphasis is on purchase as opposed to sale. Considerable time and research is spent on choosing a share. This ensures that more likely than not the selection would be good.
4. As considerable time is spent in researching the company before the share is purchased and the investments held are likely to be in a number of companies, the risks are likely to be lower.
5. Long term investments are better as a rule for family persons and other non-professional investors as they do not have the means or usually the facility or the ability of reacting quickly enough.

~

Chapter 21

~

Speculation

The word "speculate" is explained in the dictionary as "consider, form opinions (without having complete knowledge), guess, buy and sell goods, stocks and shares, etc. with risk of loss and hope of profit through changes in the market value." It is because of the risk of loss that Mark Twain cautioned individuals, "October. This is one of the peculiarly dangerous months to speculate in stocks. The others are July, January, September, April, November, May, March, June, December, August and February."

Mark Twain notwithstanding, the stock market and the possibility of instant wealth has excited men from the time the first stock exchange began in 1611 in a roofless courtyard in Amsterdam. De La Vega at that time called it "this gambling hell" and observed that "it is foolish to think you can withdraw from the exchange after you have tasted to sweetness of the honey." This is true. The exchange is addictive and once you have made a profit or even ventured into the market, it is impossible to withdraw.

David Dreman after a study of speculation states, "Four general principles seem to emerge from a study of financial speculations. First, an irresistible image of instant wealth is always presented that draws a financial crowd into existence. Second, a social reality is created that brings most people to the dangers of the mania. Opinions converge and become facts. Experts become leaders strongly exhorting the crowds on. Overconfidence becomes dominant and standards of conduct and experience of many years quickly forgotten. Third, the Le Bon image of the magic lantern suddenly changes and anxiety replaces overconfidence. The distended bubble breaks with an ensuing panic. And fourth, we do not, as investors, learn from past mistakes — things really do seem very different each time, although in fact each set of circumstances are remarkably similar to the last."

Until the Harshad Mehta scam the market was driven by speculation. Then there was a lull and the market again rose rapidly in 2006 till the financial meltdown plunged the market. At the time the Sensex had hit 30,000 and there was wild speculation that it would rise to 50,000 and 60,000. After the market plunged to below 10,000, the retail investor fled the market to surface again in 2014 when the Bharatiya Janata Party swept the elections. Speculation was again rife and the growth of the market for the first twelve months was significant. Rumours again abounded that the Sensex would rise by 50%.

Speculation is exciting. It is here to stay. However, all speculators are not successful. Several lose fortunes. As a speculator, apart from remembering Syrus' comment, "Everything is worth what its purchaser will pay for it," a few other points should be considered.

You Should Have Enough Money

A speculator must have enough money to play the market. Without money he cannot speculate or take positions in the expectations of price rises. Without money he would be forced to square positions that he has taken — sometimes at a loss.

Use Spare Cash for Speculation

The speculator should use money that he has spare — money he can afford to lose. If he is using the money he has saved to buy a house or a car to speculate, he will be under a lot of pressure to make a profit or to sell the shares if they begin to fall. Only if the speculator can afford to lose the money will he have the mental freedom to take the necessary risks. And taking well-calculated risks is the key to successful speculating.

Have Patience

In successful speculation, as in investing, profits are made by determining trends and then waiting for them to unfold. This is difficult to do. But this control is necessary for an operator to make money. If a speculator believes the price will rise he will buy and wait till it rises. He will not worry about momentary fluctuations. Similarly in a bull market he will buy and hold onto shares until the time he feels the prices will turn and begin to fall.

Determine the Big Picture

The successful speculator spends his time determining the big picture — what will happen — will the market rise or will it fall? He buys on the basis of his analysis. The speculator's aim is not to buy as cheap as possible but to buy as prices are rising. While accumulating, each purchase will normally be at a higher price than the earlier one. When shares are sold each sale will be at a lower level than the previous one. Speculators maintain that share prices are never too high to begin buying or too low to begin selling so long as the trend is interpreted properly. The speculator repeats his order only if his analysis is proved correct. Money is not made in following individual shares but by determining the trend and the way the entire market is going.

Test Before Going All-Out

If a speculator intends to buy or sell a large number of shares he must first see whether the market can take it because it can result in the price rising or falling tremendously. If he wants to buy, say 1,00,000 shares, he should buy slowly, in lots of 5,000 and 10,000 so that there is no perceptible buying trend. If he buys the whole lot in three days or so, the price will rise disproportionately and then if he sells the amount accumulated — the market may not be able to absorb so much supply, or the shares will plunge to a very low price.

Don't Be in a Hurry

A speculator will not buy in a hurry. He always waits till he notices a trend and then acts accordingly. He will not sell until he is sure the prices will fall. Similarly, he will not buy until he is sure prices will rise. He will not buy just because prices appear low. He will wait till the trend is confirmed.

Follow Your Own Hunch, Not the Crowd's

The speculator follows his judgement. He will not buy or sell because everyone else is doing so. He will not allow himself to be influenced by the opinions of others because if he does he might change the stance he has taken after analysing the market and that can be dangerous.

Don't Add to a Loss

If after buying a share, the price falls then the speculator will not normally add more to his portfolio as his assessment of the trend is not correct. This is contrary to the principle of averaging where some would buy when prices fall, to average costs. Averaging according to the speculator, is risky as the price may continue to fall.

Accept Losses

A speculator is not afraid to take losses. If the price is falling and in his opinion the share will continue to fall he will sell even if it is at a loss and thereby cut his losses. He will not let it ride in the hope that the price will eventually rise.

Take Prompt Action

Speculators act promptly. Prices rise and fall very fast. One does not necessarily have the luxury of dawdling — procrastinating whether to buy or not. Successful speculators act decisively once they have perceived a trend.

Professionalise Deals

The successful speculator is a professional. His head rather than his heart makes the trading decision. His transactions are not based on optimism but on analysis and perception.

Taking Time off

Like all professionals, the speculator needs to take a vacation — a break from the serious business of buying and selling shares. He needs to take time off to examine his position and assess the market. If he does not take time off he will not be able to take a detached overview of the market or even to freshen his mind.

Bulls Die, Too

A bull market cannot continue for ever. It has to end at some time. This normally happens when it is overheated and prices have risen beyond logical reasons. The successful speculator begins to sell when a whisper of a bear trend begins. Experienced speculators actually begin to buy when a bull market is anticipated and begin to sell when it becomes a fact.

Buying Shares at Historic Lows

A share which is trading at its historic low is a good share to buy especially if it is of a company that is performing well. It then has the potential of rising. It is these shares that speculators tend to purchase in large numbers.

Believing in Oneself

A speculator has to believe in himself and his own judgement. If he does not and instead listens to everyone around him, he is bound to be confused. Decisions made will be coloured and not as a result of reasoned thought.

Learn from Errors

Man is human and will err. The factor that distinguishes man from beast is that he can learn from these mistakes and ensure that he does not make the same mistakes again. Successful speculators analyse the causes of their mistakes and do not repeat them.

Don't Think About Tops and Bottoms

A successful speculator never attempts to buy at the very bottom or sell at the very top. He knows tops and bottoms are momentary and that it is impossible at the best of times to determine when it will be the top or the bottom. He always buys when prices are ascending and sells when prices descending. In short, a speculator is not greedy and does not try to squeeze the last drop of profit.

Reversing Positions

When a speculator is in a losing position he does not sell everything immediately as he could have a double loss — losing when the market goes down, and then losing more when the market goes up.

History Repeats Itself

A speculator knows that history always repeats itself. Prices will rise, then fall, and then rise again. So if the price falls he knows it will rise again in time.

Triangle Trading

When prices are moving up, the speculator's purchase is likened to a triangle. He initially may buy 4000 shares of XYZ, then another 3000 shares, then 2000 shares more, and so on. His purchases are highest when the market is at the lowest levels. He can also change positions faster. He will, when he sells, sell more at the higher price and then sell progressively less in future transactions. By doing so he protects himself against minor market reversals.

Follow the Leader

All shares do not move together in one direction. However, all the shares of one group or industry do move up in a bull market and down in a bear market. Thus, a speculator would observe the direction of the industry leader and then purchase or sell shares of others in the industry.

Speculation will always be there in the markets and a speculator can make a lot of money. This must not be construed that a speculator is always right. He makes wrong calculations, too. However, as Bernard Baruch said, "if a speculator is correct half the time, he is batting a good average."

~

Chapter 22

~

Prices and the Price Earnings (P/E) Ratio

In December 2015, the market value of Kotak Mahindra Bank was ₹ 702. Its earnings per share were ₹ 9.56. At the same time, the market value of YES Bank were ₹ 720. However, its earnings per share were ₹ 53.73. HDFC Bank Ltd. had a market value at this time of ₹ 1,079. However its earnings per share were ₹ 44.26.

Now,

- Why are the prices so different?
- Why are Kotak Mahindra shares higher priced?
- What would be a reasonable price to purchase either of these shares?

The issue boils down to what determines the price of a share? In normal circumstances this is really determined, by the investing public's confidence in the company, their belief in its future prospects, the ability and competence of its management and the expected future earnings of the company. A company whose shares are priced high is expected to earn a higher profit and a higher earning per share than another not so highly priced.

A tool that is used by analysts, financial experts and investors to check whether shares are reasonably priced is the price earnings ratio or the P/E ratio as it is often termed. This ratio is extremely popular and widely used as it reduces to an arithmetical figure the relationship between market price and the earnings per share and thereby creates the opportunity to make comparisons between shares. One can use it to determine whether a share is overpriced or underpriced and it enables one to assess the period of time it would take to recover one's investment.

Above all, the P/E ratio reflects the opinion of the investing public about the company — whether the company is growing or at a decline, whether the price of the share is likely to leap, remain stagnant, or fall.

The P/E ratio is arrived at by dividing the price or market value of a share by the earnings per share (profit after tax and preference dividend divided by the number of shares issued by their company —*see* Illustration 22.1).

Illustration 22.1

Pudina Limited is a company involved in the export of textiles to Europe and North America. Its shareholders funds on 31 December 2015 were as follows:

	(₹ 000s)
200,000 ordinary share of ₹ 10 each	2,000
100,000 10% preference shares of ₹ 10 each	1,000
Reserves	5,000
	₹ 8,000

The profit that the company had made after tax for the calendar and financial year 2015 was ₹ 1,500,000.
The market price of the share on 31 December 2015 was ₹ 105.

(a) The earning per share would be:

Earnings	1,500,000
Less dividend on pref. shares	- 100,000
Earnings for ordinary shareholders	1,400,000

Earnings per share $\frac{1,400,000}{200,000} = ₹ 7$

(b) The price earning (P / E) ratio would be $\frac{105}{7} = 15$

This can be taken to mean that it would take 15 years to recoup the investment made through the earnings per share that a company makes.

If it takes 15 years to recoup the investment made that suggests that the return per annum would be 6.67% per annum. The question that immediately springs to mind is why anyone would wish to invest in a share that would give only such small return, coupled with the inherent risks of the share falling in value, when one can invest one's money in totally risk free savings, such as the Public Provident Fund which guarantees tax free income at a higher rate p.a. The investor or the speculator pays a high price because he believes that for the risks he takes the return would be higher. If he expects a return of 20% p.a. he believes that the price of shares of Pudina Ltd. would increase in a year to ₹ 126. Assuming that the earnings also grow at a rate of 20% p.a. the earnings per share would be ₹ 8.5. The P/E ratio would then be 15. If however, the price remains constant the P/E would have fallen to 12 (*see* Table 22.1).

The P/E ratio is high so long as the investing public has faith in a company's ability to grow and to earn, which leads to an appreciation in its share price. The P/E ratio will fall as soon as this confidence disappears in the earning capacity of the company. This is why share prices rise dramatically in periods of boom, and fall drastically in periods of depression.

Table 22.1

Future Price of a Share at Different Earnings Growth

Price of Share	Earnings Growth	Price After 1st Yr	2nd Yr	3rd Yr
1	10%	1.10	1.21	1.33
1	11%	1.11	1.23	1.37
1	13%	1.12	1.25	1.40
1	13%	1.13	1.28	1.44
1	14%	1.14	1.30	1.48
1	15%	1.15	1.32	1.52
1	16%	1.16	1.35	1.56
1	17%	1.17	1.37	1.60
1	18%	1.18	1.39	1.64
1	19%	1.19	1.42	1.69
1	20%	1.20	1.44	1.73
1	25%	1.25	1.56	1.95
1	30%	1.30	1.69	2.20

The price that a person pays to purchase a share is based on the future prospects of a company and its anticipated earnings. In this there is a fault in the calculation of the price earnings ratio in that the calculation is made on the current market value and the earnings of the previous year. This can, however, be corrected to an extent by basing one's calculations on the estimate of current and future years earnings. This can, of course, be difficult for the general public as they may not be aware of all the plans the company has; the decisions it has made and the likes. Good sources of information to get some details are the annual report of the company and the investment media which give some excellent insights into the workings and the future of various companies.

The market is a very vibrant entity and so there are continuous upturns and downturns. The P/E of a company is therefore constantly changing. Suppose that in November 2015, the market price of a share of a hypothetical company Nivya Ltd. was ₹ 200. Its earning per share was ₹ 20. P/E was therefore, 10. In December 2015, the market price rose to ₹ 220 resulting in a P/E of 11. This tends to confuse an investor. Is the price too high? What is the fair price? Why has the price risen? Is it likely to rise more?

The safest and probably most liquid investment a person could make is the placing of a deposit in a scheduled bank which could earn a return of around 7% p.a.

The P/E of this is effectively 14 (₹ 100 divided by 7%)

The moral of this is that for extremely safe and almost risk free investments the P/E should not exceed 10, i.e. one should recover one's initial investment in no longer than 10 years. The question that arises then is what would be a fair P/E that for an investment that bears elements of risk.

Investments in shares are risky as anyone who has lived through the downslides of 1983 and 1987, or who has read of the Black Monday of October 1987 in New York, would confirm. But then why invest? The answer is elementary. The rewards and returns of investing on account of the risks are greater. And, of course, there is the excitement. The possibility exists of doubling, tripling and even quadrupling one's money in a relatively short time. On 16 June 2015, for example, the price of an Asian Paints share was ₹ 699. On 16 December 2015, the same share was quoted at ₹ 875 and that too after a dividend payout — an increase of 25% in 6 months. No deposit in a bank can beat that return.

What P/E, then, is reasonable? The market price of share is arrived at on the basis of a number of factors, the major ones being:

- The company — its management, growth, its prospects and the industry the company operates in.
- The rate the company's earnings are likely to grow at and the dividend policy of the company.
- The demand for the shares of the company. If a person is attempting a takeover, the prices will rise.
- The rate the market expects the share to grow.

The parameters under which two individuals view a share will be different — the return they wish, the prospects, and the like. Consequently, the price they are prepared to pay would differ.

Let us assume that the price of a share of Malini Bearings Ltd. (Hypothetical company) is ₹ 20. The company is growing and it is anticipated that the price would rise to ₹ 40 per share in 3 years. There are two investors — Raman & Ravi.

Ravi wants to double his investment in 3 years.

Raman wants to triple his investment in 3 years.

In this situation, Ravi would be prepared to pay the ₹ 20 per share whereas Raman would not be prepared to pay more than ₹ 13.3. In this example, for convenience the earnings per share has been considered to bring out the point that the price one is prepared to pay is directly related to the return he anticipates.

In short, the P/E that is considered reasonable is one that fulfils one's investment return requirement, which would be based on the company's projected earnings. In this it would be wise to remember that a P/E of 20 or over can normally be justified only if a company has a high growth rate (say at least 10% p.a.)

The 60% rule is a guide that can be used to decide on whether to invest in a share. The 60% rule submits that one should not purchase a share in a company at a P/E that is more than 60% of the growth anticipated. Thus, if the earning of Homedale Petrochemicals is anticipated to grow at 25% p.a., the purchase price should not exceed a P/E of 15.

Table 22.2
P/E Forecast Table

Annual Growth (Rate in %)	First Year		Second Year		Third Year	
	Earning	P/E at 40% Appreciation	Earning	P/E at 70% Appreciation	Earnings	P/E at 100% Appreciation
10	1.10	12.7	1.21	14.0	1.33	15.0
11	1.11	12.6	1.23	13.8	1.37	14.6
12	1.12	12.5	1.25	13.6	1.40	14.3
13	1.13	12.4	1.28	13.3	1.44	13.8
14	1.14	12.3	1.30	13.1	1.48	13.5
15	1.15	12.2	1.32	12.9	1.52	13.2
16	1.16	12.1	1.35	12.6	1.56	12.8
17	1.17	11.0	1.37	12.4	1.60	12.5
18	1.18	11.9	1.39	12.2	1.64	12.2
19	1.19	11.8	1.42	12.0	1.69	11.8
20	1.20	11.7	1.44	11.8	1.73	11.6
25	1.25	11.2	1.56	10.9	1.95	10.3
30	1.30	10.8	1.69	10.1	2.20	9.1

Table 22.2 illustrates the P/E one may pay in first year, second year and third year at different growth levels based on the assumption the price of the share will rise by 40% in the first year, by a further 30% in the second, and would double in value in the third year.

Thus, for example, if Nivya Ltd. is expected to grow at a rate of 15% p.a. and one expects a capital appreciation of 70% in 2 years, the P/E ratio at the end of 2 years would be 12.9.

Most shares, especially with change in the law governing capital gains tax, are being sold nowadays after a year. Table 22.3 attempts to illustrate the P/E at the end of a year at different rates of growth and different levels of capital appreciation.

It is expected that Divya Ltd. will grow at a rate of 25% p.a. Its shares are forecasted to appreciate by 30% at the end of the first year. Its P/E at the end of the first year would be 10.4.

Table 22.3
Short Term P/E Table

Rate of Annual Growth	Earnings in First Year	P/E at the end of first year at different rates of capital appreciation					
		10%	20%	30%	50%	75%	100%
10	1.10	10.0	10.9	11.8	13.6	15.9	18.2
12	1.12	9.8	10.7	11.6	13.4	15.6	17.9
14	1.14	9.6	10.5	11.4	13.2	15.4	17.5
15	1.15	9.6	10.4	11.3	13.0	15.2	17.4
20	1.20	9.2	10.0	10.8	12.5	14.6	16.7
25	1.25	8.8	9.6	10.4	12.0	14.0	16.0
30	1.30	8.5	9.2	10.0	11.5	13.5	15.4

A word of caution. Future earnings are difficult, especially for the average investor to predict and are at best, estimates. Tables 22.2 and 22.3 described therefore cannot be sworn upon as there are many variables. Although the earnings might grow, the prices may not and *vice versa*. Hence, these two tables should be studied with this in mind. It is because of this that the 60% rate is much easier to use and calculate and it is usually not far wrong.

As it is difficult to predict future growth an investor would be wise to work calculations and conclusions arrived at as developments occur. It should also be remembered that it is difficult for a company to sustain for a long period the same level of growth. New, unknown and untried companies that do not have a tract record of competence have a low P/E and consequently they may appear to be attractive investments. And, they may well be, too, then before investing in these companies one should remember that they are unknown and unproven and possibly lacks investor confidence.

In conclusion the price earnings ratio reflects the reputation of a share in the market, the confidence of its shareholders and the earning potential of the company. Hence, no one should invest until one has also examined the P/E.

~

Chapter 23

~

Random Theory

J. P. Morgan the elder is reputed to have retorted to a naïve acquaintance who had ventured to ask the great man what the market was going to do, "it will fluctuate." Some shares would rise while other would fall. It is not possible to predict. As Bernard Baruch, the Wall Street wizard once remarked, "if one is correct half the time, he is hitting a good average."

The random theory of investment is based on the premise that there is no logic in share price movements; that prices will rise and fall on whims and by the manipulations of individuals and that there is no need to study trends and movements of prices prior to making an investment in shares. A share purchased at random, on a whim, literally, is likely, it is argued, to be as successful as another purchased after days of analysis and thought.

This theory, which has also been called "the great fool theory," is best illustrated by an actual happening. The editor of the *Forbes* magazine, to prove that share prices acted illogically stuck the stock market quotation pages of the *New York Times* on the wall of his office and threw ten darts. Two darts missed the target. On the basis on the eight darts that actually hit the target he invested a hypothetical $ 28,000. The prices of these hypothetical investments were monitored closely. In 15 years, they had appreciated 3.6 times whereas the capital appreciation of the share price-index of Standard and Poor had appreciated by only 2.6 times!

The random theory gained weightage from the fact that the two basic methods of predicting prices — fundamental analysis and technical analysis, are not completely accurate. An example is the huge spurt in Essar Oil from ₹ 103.9 on 16 December 2014 to ₹ 226.60 on 17 December 2015. The small turnaround in results did not warrant the price increase which was based on expectations. Analysis of part trends and figures could never reveal this. Additionally even though it is claimed "figures don't lie," creative accounting can conceal the true picture to all except the trained eye. Neither fundamental analysis nor technical analysis account for the future and this is their greatest pitfall. And as the future is hazy, the randomists say what does it matter if one chooses any particular share?

Dalal Street is not an exception to the random walk theory. Dr. Jandhyala L. Sharma, in his doctoral dissertation at the University of Arkansas in 1976, presented substantial evidence to prove that price movements at the Bombay Stock Exchange followed a random pattern. His study was based on 131 monthly observations during the period 1963-73 of the Bombay Variable Dividend Industrial Security Index published by the Reserve Bank of India. His sample was also supplemented by 268 weekly prices of 23 shares on the specified list of the Bombay Stock Exchange during 1968 to 1973. Dr. Sharma came to the conclusion that prices at the Bombay Stock Exchange showed randomness and that randomly selected shares could outperform shares picked out by cold sound logic and reasoning. This is its greatest merit.

What really are the other advantage of this theory? There are a few:

1. As shares are picked at random — without preference or evaluation or bias, the question of good or bad (or any) judgement does not arise as no judgement takes place. This makes it easier for persons who have no idea of the stock markets to invest.
2. As shares are picked at random there can be no question of following the crowd. Hence one is insulated against the dangers of the crowd being wrong.
3. The investment decision can never be ill-informed as no information is sought or consulted before the investment is made.
4. As the shares purchased are selected at random and without bias the chances of accumulating a balanced portfolio are good. As the shares are likely to cover a diversified group of companies, the investment would be protected against industry risks and cyclicality. The returns, too, are likely to be reasonable and usually above average.

However there are pitfalls:

1. The random theory lays the investment decision beyond the investor's control inasmuch as the shares purchased are chosen in a manner where the investor has no control on the share that will be chosen. As a consequence, too much dependence is placed on lady-luck and if luck is against the investor, he stands to lose a lot of money. But then randomists counter this with, "audentis fortune juvat — fortune favours the brave."
2. On a random selection it is possible for one to pick dogs or lemons — shares that have no potential or hope to grow in the foreseeable future. A friend of mine once, to test this theory; closed his eyes and placed a notation on shares of a textile machinery making company whose prices were even at that time falling. He placed ₹ 5,000 in shares of the company. It is presently a sick company. Even its debenture holders have not been paid interest.
3. The random theory is speculation at its best — the belief that prices will and must rise and that shares will rise come what may. The obvious danger is that prices could fall and one may be plain unlucky.

There are three factors to remember:

- Technical and financial analyses cannot guarantee superior returns, nor outperform a simple buy and hold strategy in the long run.
- One must diversify one's portfolio as much as possible. This eliminates the risk that is inherent in individual companies.
- The random theory also advocates the need to invest for a long period as studies have proved that the random theory is not effective in a short term.

The random theory above all vindicates that price movements cannot be predicted with certainty over a period of time and this makes the game exciting and enthralling. Throw your darts and join the game.

~

Chapter 24

~

The Value of Contrary Opinion

Bernard Baruch, the legendary Wall Street investor is credited with the statements "Be different. Buy when everyone is selling and sell when everyone is buying." This is the rule of contrary opinion and requires an investor to do exactly the opposite of what others are doing, namely sell when others are purchasing and buy when others are selling. It is based on the very sound principle of supply and demand. Prices will fall when there is an excess of supply, whether it be of shares or anything else. Therefore buying in a falling market is beneficial. Similarly when everyone is purchasing a share, the price is likely to rise as demand may exceed supply. As prices would be rising, it would be a good time to sell. The belief assumes, of course, that at a time in the future markets will rise (when prices are falling and contrarians are buying shares) and that prices are likely to fall (when prices are rising and contrarians are selling shares). During booms and bull markets, such as the one that began in 2005, the contrarians would be selling shares as fast as they can in order to purchase them again when prices begin to fall.

The philosophy of contrarians is excellently illustrated by an incident. Professors of a well-known business school in the United States sought to prove, by scientific deduction and irrefutable logic, which shares to buy and which to sell. Data regarding trends, industry studies and historical facts along with the pronouncements of accepted pundits were fed into a computer. After a while the computer came up with the answer, "Buy low, sell high." This is exactly the strategy contrarians follow. They aim to actively buy in bear phases (when prices fall) and sell during bullish phases (when prices rise). In short, a dedicated or committed contrarian does exactly the opposite of what the rest of the market does thus giving himself an opportunity to make enormous profits.

Being a contrarian is difficult because man has the mob or herd instinct. There is a tendency to do what everyone else is doing. Thus, to sell at a time when prices are soaring, is indeed very difficult. This is why there are so few contrarians.

Buying a share which no one else is buying takes guts and when this is done successfully a financial legend is born. The late Vittal Mallya became known as one of the great investors and identifiers of stock when he purchased a drastically undervalued Cadbury's. Mundra and Himmatsinghe amassed a fortune when they purchased shares of Jayant Vitamins that was floundering. And in a small way, a banker I know made a small fortune for himself when he purchased shares of PEICO (later Philips) and ACC which no one else wanted to touch. However, before you go charging to seek and buy shares that no one else wants please remember that out of every 120 contrarians only about 17 succeed. The odds against success are very great. This is because the basic assumption is that one should seek shares in troubled industries. At these times (when a company is doing badly or an industry is at a depression) investors will, sell in the belief that prices will decline. They will do this especially if profits are falling and dividends are not being declared. As they sell, others also begin to sell and the price falls steadily. The contrarian believes that at a point of time it must stop. There is a point at which the price can go down further. This could be because of the intrinsic value of the share and because there are no more sellers left. This is when the contrarian come in with the firm belief that prices have to now go up. Prices rise and he makes a profit. In a good market, the reverse holds.

The contrarian always follows certain rules:

1. The contrarian sells when others are buying expecting prices to rise and rise again. He does not wait for the price to peak but sells as soon as he makes a reasonable profit.
2. Another reason not to sell at the peak is because the person who buys must have a reason to purchase.

3. The contrarian is, and has to be, in total control and sell or buy at the decided target price. If one is greedy and waits for the highest price, the shares may fall resulting in lower profits.
4. The contrarian never looks back after a sale or purchase has been made and never wonders whether he should have waited. This is, to him, wasteful. He always looks ahead.

As far as he is concerned the main thing is to sell at a profit and to buy at a price that will ensure a profit. He never wonders whether he could have sold the share for ₹ 15 more or purchased it for ₹ 20 less. The share could easily have fallen or risen respectively. As Nathan Rothschild once said, "Sell and grow rich."

The theory of contrarian opinion works only when opinions differ. There is always the danger that the contrarian is wrong and the others correct. Contrary opinion investing to succeed requires the contrarian to be aware of what is happening in the industry, in the economy, and in the company. There is no point in purchasing shares in a company that is doing badly.

How does the contrarian decide when it's the time to buy or sell? Contrarians advise patience until one is convinced that the future would not get any worse and the fundamentals will improve. Or, if an industry is going through a depression, the contrarian must determine when the up swing will be. He invests with the knowledge that he may be wrong. In short, contrarians require patience, money and a lot of guts.

The great danger in any market is that there may be a number of contrarians. If there are, then the benefits of contrary opinion would be negated to an extent. Initially, and until a majority develops, it is better to be a part of the crowd. When the majority begins to dominate, it is then that one should be a contrarian. As Keynes once wrote, "Worldly wisdom teaches that it is better for reputation to gain conventionally than to succeed unconventionally."

~

Chapter 25

~

Evergreen or Buy and Hold Strategy

The evergreen strategy is based on the premise that share prices will keep rising. It is appropriate in countries such as India where historically share prices have always been rising at a level higher than inflation. Additionally, in India we usually do have the phenomenon of "too much money chasing too few shares." Mutual funds are bloated with cash. There are also billions of dollars being invested by foreign institutional investors (FIIs). Consequently, the chances are that prices will keep rising although there may be technical corrections from time to time. The main thing that the evergreen strategist has to do is to determine whether the trend is one of rising prices. And if it is, he should buy and keep, and buy some more. As Jean Paul Getty, arguably one of the greatest strategists of all time, said, "Bank on the trends and do not worry about the tremors. Keep your mind on long term cycles and ignore the sporadic ups and downs."

The evergreen strategy does not work when prices are falling or if prices are not rising at all. Prices have to be rising in the long term.

The strategist buys shares and holds them. These shares would be of companies that are growing and profitable and ones that are committed to long term growth. The strategist buys the shares and waits (even for years) as the shares double and treble in value or as Peter

Lynch, the author of "One Up on Wall Street" would call them "ten baggers."

The evergreen strategist does not buy into just one company. He would buy into several growing companies in different industries thus hedging his risks. As he is convinced prices will rise, he would normally buy additional quantity whenever prices fall. He would not normally sell shares to make a quick profit or if prices have fallen momentarily. This is because, as stated earlier, he hopes to make his money by the growth of a company and not by aberrations in the market.

The main thing and the factor most difficult in this strategy is to determine which share to buy because on this rests success or failure. After doing this, one must decide how much to buy, when to buy and at what price.

Once that is done, the strategist buys shares. Although he may not sell every time the price peaks, he always buys when the price falls. The companies he normally invests in are those that plough back a large amount of their profits for expansion and growth. Dividends paid out are low. Consequently, gains made are from capital appreciation and not dividend income.

As the evergreenist's strategy is to buy shares and keep them, he saves on brokerage fees. He does not also have to wait for long periods to get his money. He has money and is prepared to bide his time. He does not normally need to quickly turn it around. Hence, he does not normally bother to encash his gains or sell to cut his losses. He is prepared to ride along for long term profits. If shares of good companies have been chosen well, then losses are likely to be less than 40 to 50 per cent whereas profits can be as high as one's luck is — a 1,000 per cent gain is not improbable.

The key to success in this strategy is the choice of a share.

The criteria to be considered are:

1. Choose a good, fundamentally strong company;
2. Choose a company in a high growth industry;
3. Do not place all your monies in one company but in a number of companies and in different industries;
4. Avoiding speculative shares;

5. Purchase shares over a period of time so that market tremors are evened out; and
6. Do not be impatient. Do not expect quick results. Conversely, if the market dips a little, do not sell in panic. The aim is long term profits.

It is good to purchase and keep shares. But profits are not made until they are encashed. And there are times when the evergreenists must also sell shares:

1. If a share has made a large loss or if it is felt that choosing a particular share was a mistake then it should be sold.
2. If a company is no longer growing and its long term future is uncertain then its shares should be disposed of.
3. If the price earning ratio exceeds 35 and the price of the share has doubled in 12 months, it should be sold as the growth may not be as fast in the future.

The main thing to remember is that this is a long term strategy. One is not in it for quick gains. A study done recently revealed that more money is being made by the evergreenists than by any other group of investors.

~

Chapter 26

~

Fundamental Approach

Nemish Shah, a broker in Mumbai. advises investors to purchase shares with good fundamentals. So do many others. The theory they are propounding is known as the fundamental approach to the purchase of shares and is based on the premise that "figures don't lie."

This approach to purchasing shares submits that one should not purchase shares without first studying in detail all matters that are relevant to the company whose shares one proposes to buy. This study would involve examining its sales, earnings, profit margins, dividends, management proficiency, industrial and business outlook, labour competence and any other factor that could have a bearing on its performance in the future. On the basis of such a study fundamentalists believe that they can project a company's future profits and earnings capacity with reasonable accuracy. They then use these projections to estimate what the price of a company's shares ought to be. This estimated price is known or termed as the share's true or intrinsic value. Once this figure has been arrived at, it is compared with the present market value. There will be a difference between the estimated intrinsic value and the present market value.

The fundamentalists believe that the price will either move up or down to reduce this difference or gap.

If the estimated intrinsic value is higher than the market value, it is believed that the prices will rise. In this situation fundamentalists will purchase shares as this difference presents them with an opportunity to make profits. The greater the difference, the greater the opportunity to make a profit.

Alternatively if the intrinsic value is lower than the market value, the share is overpriced and is an indication to the fundamentalist to sell.

Let us take the instance of Kumar and D'Souza, a hypothetical engineering firm. Its shares are quoted at ₹ 58. Its profits were handsome and its growth has been at about 30 per cent per annum. The industry average is only 24 per cent. The general outlook is good, its management is competent and it is believed that the company will maintain its performance. On this basis the intrinsic value of a share was estimated at ₹ 72. In this situation fundamentalists believe that the shares would rise to ₹ 72 and the ₹ 14 (difference between the intrinsic value and the market price) represents the profit potential in each share of Kumar and D'Souza. Conversely if the intrinsic value was estimated at ₹ 45, it would be believed that the shares are highly overpriced and that the market price would move down to ₹ 45. Consequently, the fundamentalist will sell the shares he holds to avoid or avert a loss:

- The approach though sound and based on financial figures does suffer from some drawbacks and to make this approach work effectively one must be aware of them.
- It tends to ignore market sentiment and assumes that the market will act rationally. The market seldom does. Prices flare or drop on the flimsiest of reasons.
- The fundamental approach is based on a rational and scientific analysis of data. The market is rarely rational.
- The information and analysis itself may be incorrect.
- Many companies disguise real earning with the help of creative / innovative accounting and accounting cosmetics.
- The fundamentalists estimate of intrinsic value may be incorrect. This is not only possible but more probable than not as he has to often forecast growth, profit and other factors without having all the facts in his grasp.
- The fundamentalists may not fully understand the economy or the industry as there are several external factors.

- There is also the possibility that the market may not move in the manner of a fundamentalist expects and conversely towards the intrinsic value.
- It is also difficult to determine corporate action.

In short, if the fundamental approach is used as a means to make profits by buying underpriced shares then that route is fraught with problems. However, the principle can be used effectively to purchase shares of strong and viable companies and the financial and other factors must be studied in detail before shares are purchased. Kumar, an investment fund manager in Mumbai, voiced his investment theory thus "I buy shares of only financially strong companies that are growing. I first look at its profit, growth, its sales growth, its dividend history and its profit plough back. Next I look at its share capital and its reserves. If I like them I look further at product range, management and other factors. If I still like it I buy. I do not buy for short term gains but because I believe in the company and because I believe the money is safe."

This really is the crux of the matter. The fundamental approach works exceedingly well in determining the intrinsic value of a company. It is not such an effective tool in determining future price movements and hence it is not very dependable for short term profits. An investor ignores the fundamental approach however at his peril because it is imperative that no investment be made without examining the strengths of a company. A friend of mine several years ago, at the word of a friend, purchased shares in a Hyderabad based company, Gangappa Cables at ₹ 11 per share. He knew nothing of the company then and knows nothing of it now. All he does know is that the share is no longer quoted on any stock exchange and that his investment is a dead loss.

~

Chapter 27

~

The Technical Approach

Sanatan Gandhi, an analyst friend of mine rang me up the other day to inform me "the resistance has been broken and that a reaction is to set in soon." This may sound like goobledygook to many. Sanatan, however, is a firm believer in technical analysis and he was conveying to me that the market which had stubbornly stayed at a particular level for some time was going to move upwards. In technical analysis a reaction means a movement upwards.

Technical analysis is a tool used to determine which shares one should buy and which one should sell. The analysis attempts to predict the future price of a share on the basis of a study of its price movements in the past. In doing so it ignores fundamental data such as earnings, profit margins, management competence, industry conditions and economic factors as it is argued that these factors are already reflected in the market price of a share. The assumption is that all factors that can affect the price of the share — fundamental, political, psychological and the likes have already been taken into consideration by the market operators. It is also assumed that they have considered present and expected performance and that the present market price of a share reflects the collective opinion of the investing public of the share price. There is some truth in this as the market is usually aware of a company's performance and the industry within which it operates.

The trend in prices is the basis of technical analysis. Charts are prepared to determine trends and to determine whether prices are likely to rise or to fall. The key in this approach is to identify trends in their early stages of development in order to trade in the direction of those trends. If the trend is that the price of ABC Limited would rise, one would purchase it in anticipation of a price rise and consequent profits. Alternatively, if it is believed that a share will fall, the technical analyst would just sell them. The premise here is that prices move in trends and that a trend is more likely to continue than to reverse.

Benjamin Franklin is credited for having said, "Show me the man who does not believe in history and I will show you a fool." Technical analysts believe in history, and, also that history repeats itself. Consequently all their predictions and charts are based on history. Past figures and trends are used to predict the future.

Technical analysts maintain that the price of a share at any time (present price) is the balance then struck by buyers and sellers. Price movements take place on account of changes in buying or selling pressures. This occurs on account of diverse internal and external factors, such as profits, political environment, predictions and the likes. Prices stabilize when an equilibrium between buyers and sellers is achieved. They believe that a record of price movements over a period of time depicts how investors (both buyers and sellers) have acted and behaved over a period of time in the past. As the whole theory is based on the assumption that history repeats itself, the approach submits that human nature does not change and that man is likely to repeat his pattern of past behaviour in the future. It is believed that this record of past movements will repeat themselves in the future.

The main weakness of this theory is the assumption that past pattern of price behaviour will repeat itself in the future. There is little or no evidence to support this. It is also extremely difficult logically to support this statement. A company's prices may be on the ascendant for several reasons. There is no reason to claim or argue that this trend would continue in the foreseeable future. This is especially true in situations when the affairs of a company take a down turn. Additionally, after a bull market prices can fall sharply. Technical analysis does not take this into account.

Another factor that technical analysts do not consider is the fundamentals of a company — its sales, earnings, reserves, assets, growth, liquidity and the likes. It deals solely with movement which is very often irrational. In the long run — and this has been proven time and again — it is better to purchase shares of companies that are fundamentally strong.

Price movements give an indication of the parameters within which a share has moved during a period of time (12 months or 6 months) and this is valuable information. It indicates the price up to which it has demonstrated its potential to rise and the depths to which it has sunk. Theoretically, therefore, if one purchases a share within that band he cannot lose as it has the ability to rise up to its highest recorded price. The lower the price at which one purchases the share within the band, the greater is the possibility of higher profits.

Another great advantage of technical analysis is that it is based on actual price movements in the market and it is not on anticipated or forecasted estimates. It takes into account human nature and the laws of demand and supply.

In conclusion, technical analysis is a useful tool in determining possible price movements. However, it must not be relied on solely — one must also examine the strengths and weaknesses of the company and the industry within which it operates.

~

Chapter 28

~

Dow Theory

The Foundation of Technical Analysis

The study on stock markets and price movements first published by Charles H. Dow on 3 July 1884 is the most popular and the most quoted of stock market theories and it forms the basis of all technical studies. This theory concerns itself solely with the stock market — the movement of share prices and nothing else. It does not concern itself with facets of the companies concerned, such as the competence of the management, the quality of its products and the likes. It deals purely with movements and prices.

Consequently, a criticism that is often leveled at this theory is that the signals are given "too late." But then, Dow did not intend that his findings be used to forecast movements. His submission was only that share prices move in trends. Once this submission is accepted, it can be used as a guide to price trends and with a "touch of salt" extrapolated to predict movements. It is because of this ability that the Dow Theory, as it is popularly known, has remained the basis of technical analysis.

The Dow Theory also holds that the shares of companies in an industry go up or down together. This is why companies are grouped together by industry in technical analysis. The suggestion is that like must be compared with like; unlikes will differ. Exceptions to the movements of industrial averages, though they do exist, are not very common and do not persist for any length of time. While in periods of depression some share prices may fall faster than others, and in periods of boom some prices may rise faster than others, most shares will move in concert with each other. The exceptions (those that rise or fall faster) too will stabilize in time.

The following are the important propositions of the Dow Theory:

Average Discounts Everything

Share prices have taken into account every imaginable factor — political, economic, supply, demand the likes. In early 2015, for example, in anticipation that Greece would leave the Eurozone, the markets plunged only to recover when it did not. In December 2015, in anticipation of the US Fed raising interest rates the market adjusted itself. The anticipation was an increase of 0.5%. However, on 16 December 2015 the raise in the rate was only 0.25%, the market reacted sharply and the Sensex went up by 287 points.

Market Trends

The Dow Theory states that there are three price trends — the primary, the secondary and the tertiary trend and that these co-exist at the same time.

Before one goes any further, it is important to look at two basic factors — uptrend and downtrend. An uptrend exists so long as each successive price high is higher than the previous one, and each successive price low is higher than the one before. A downtrend is exactly the opposite. This definition of uptrend and downtrend forms the basis of trend analysis.

With regard to the three trends, the most important is the primary trend. It is a broad-based upward or downward swing usually lasting for a year to several years. It is believed to reflect the basic mood in the market and consequently, for the proponents of this theory, the primary trend is the basis for successful investing. In the uptrend each new peak is higher than the earlier one. In the downtrend each low is below the previous one. A discerning investor, once he establishes that an upward trend has started would continue to buy shares until he receives a clear indication that the trend has reversed.

The secondary or intermediate trend represents corrections in the primary trend and usually lasts for a month to around three to four months. The corrections reverse about a third to two-thirds of the earlier trend. A more aggressive investor would normally trade in the secondary trend. The minor or tertiary trend lasts from a few hours to less than a month (usually 20 days) and accounts for short term price movements. These are for the trader — the man who is in the ring — not for long term investors.

The theory symbolizes fluctuations in share prices to tides, waves and ripples. The mood of the sea — the strength of the tide — is likened to the rise or fall in the prices. As long as the peak of each wave is higher than the previous peak and the trough is higher than the earlier one, it is assumed that the tide is rising. In a falling tide, the reverse is true. The peak is lower than the earlier peak and the trough is lower than the earlier trough.

Trends are useful in forecasting. It is useful to know how the trends are moving; where the trends have gone up to and where it is likely to go to. As there can be several, a discerning investor should be careful in the choosing of trends.

Trends

Each trend has three clear phases. In an upward or bullish market, the first phase is known as the accumulation phase. This is the time when discerning investors or the early birds begin buying as they perceive that prices will begin to move up. In the second phase, trend followers begin to notice an upward or bullish trend and begin to start buying. Prices begin to improve and advance very fast and word begins to get around. In the third and final phase, the general public begins to buy shares and prices begin to soar. It is at this last stage that the discerning early birds who had bought shares at low prices begin to sell them. In a bearish phase, on the other hand, astute investors perceive the markets will fall and begin selling. They are joined at the second stage by the trend watchers. In the last stage, there is panic and everyone sells.

Averages Conform to Each Other

The theory submits that averages in general move in concert. The averages in different industries will move up or low at around the same time. No major bear or bull market movements will occur unless averages also move in a similar manner. This is true. In the bull boom of 1990, the prices of all shares and in different industries soared together. At the end of 1990, they fell together too.

Volume Confirms Trends

Volumes, or the number of shares sold or bought, confirms the trend. In a bullish market, more and more shares will be bought, whereas in a bearish market, the volumes of shares sold will be on the ascendant.

Ongoing Trend Will Continue Till There are Clear Indications that It is Changing

This suggests that until there is a clear indication that a trend is changing, one should assume that it is continuing. If the market is bullish, one should not sell before one is certain that the trend has changed and prices are about to fall. Conversely, should not begin to buy in a bear market until one is sure that there are clear indications or signals that the prices are beginning to rise. This rule warns against one changing positions too soon. It recognizes this and expects investors to realize that nothing remains the same. The price will go up and it will go down. It never remains stationary. Booms or bull markets have to end some time. So do bear markets. The investor has to watch trends and act when a reversal is clear.

To put the theory into practice is to be able to determine at what stage one should buy and at what stage one should sell.

As soon as prices rise, some investors will sell, causing share price to move from a peak to a trough. As prices dip a little more investors will, in a bullish market, begin to buy, causing the prices to rise again. This will continue in a bull market and Figure 28.1 and Figure 28.2 on next page highlight positions when shares could be sold.

In Figure 28.1, the peak O is below peak M. The trough P is much below trough N. The sale point should be considered R.

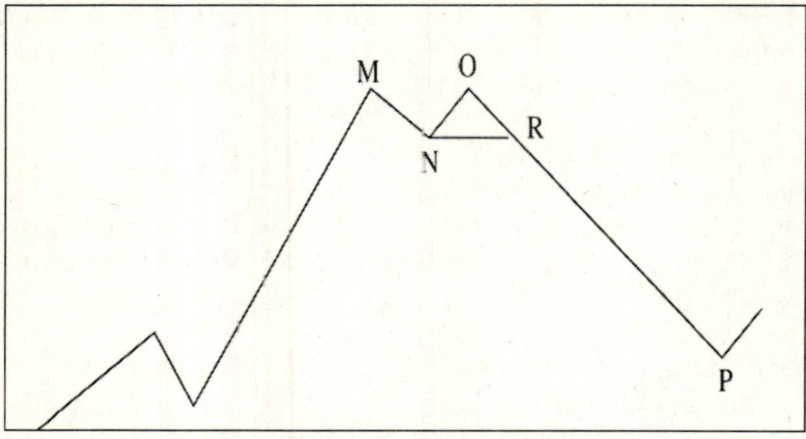

Figure 28.1: R is the point to sell in a bull Market

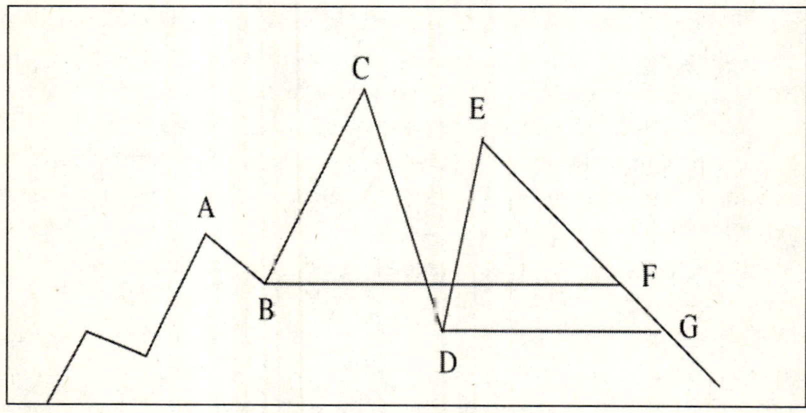

Figure 28.2: Sell at F and G levels

In Figure 28.2, the peak C is higher than peak A. However, peak E is lower than peak C. Trough B is higher than trough D. The selling can take place preferably, if one is quick at point F and definitely at point G.

What above bear markets? When should one begin to buy?

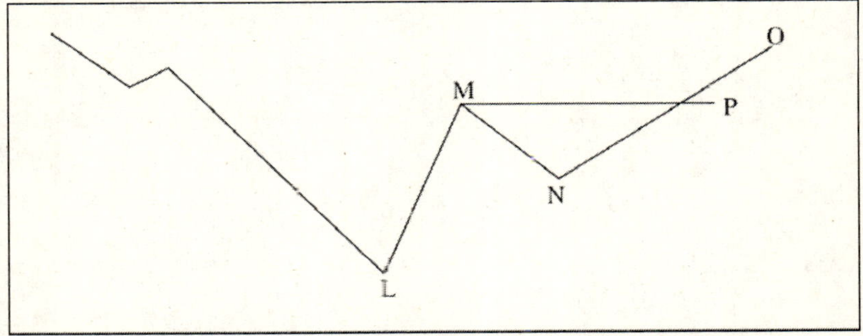

Figure 28.3: Level P in the place to buy in an ascending market

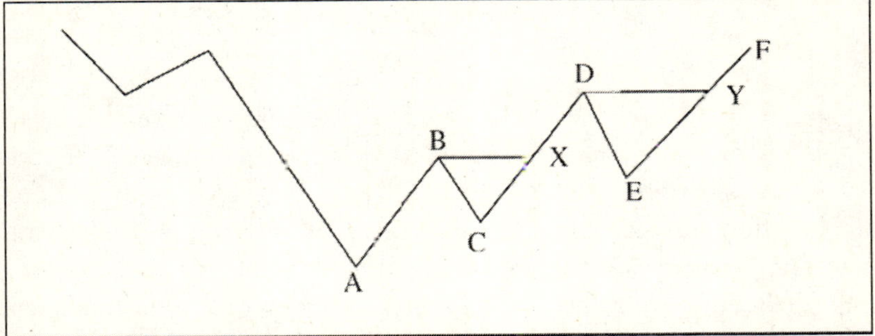

Figure 28.4: In an ascending market, X and Y are the points to buy

The trough L in Figure 28.3 is lower than trough N, and the peak O is higher than peak M. The time to buy would be at level P which is, in effect, the price at peak M.

In an ascending market, as trough C is higher than trough A, and as peak B is lower than peak D, the indication to buy will be at X in the first instance — *see* Figure 28.4. Similarly, as peak F is higher than peak D, the second buy signal will be at Y.

While the Dow Theory can predict uptrends or downtrends the criticism that is leveled at it is that the signals are too delayed. A peak and a trough have to be completed before the signal can be taken. Also, one can often miss the signals.

Still it has to be accepted that the Dow Theory has proved itself to be a good guide to price movements and the basic premises of the theory are logical and reasonable. It is because of this that this Dow Theory is the cornerstone of technical analysis.

Chapter 29

~

Elliot Wave Theory

"Buy now" Vijay Kumar castigated me in November 2015. "The index will hit 40,000 before the budget." Another expert told me to sell as there was no rational explanation for the rise in share prices. Newspapers, magazines and analysts predict lower future trends, often without basis. Frequently the predictions are right. More often they are wrong. And those who predict correctly more often than others become cult figures and investors hang on to their every word — confident of stupendous gains. Ah! To foresee the future.

One theory for predicting share prices is the Elliot Wave Theory which is a variation of technical analysis and is considered by its adherents to be an improvement on the Dow Theory. Consequently, several market men use the Elliot Wave Theory to confirm trends thrown up by the Dow Theory.

The Elliot Wave Theory is the brainchild of Mr. R.N. Elliot, an accountant. After his retirement and while ill, he lay in bed and studied share price movements and charts. He discerned a noticeable order or pattern in price movements. He propounded that share prices went up or down in waves. This theory was further developed by Collins, Frost, Proctor and Beckman and came to be known as the Elliot Wave Theory.

The theory classifies share price movements into two basic moves.

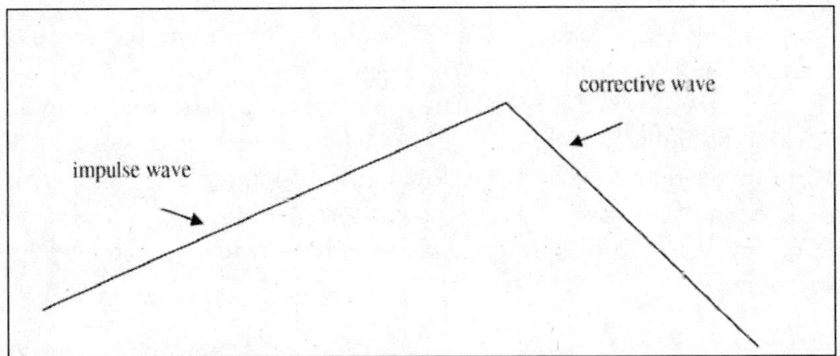

Figure 29.1: The two basic moves according to Elliot Wave Theory – impulse wave and corrective wave

The first is the up move when price go "up" and is called impulse. The second is predictably called "down" and is called the corrective. Figure 29.1 illustrates the two movements. It would be observed and appreciated that while the impulse (up) is gradual and takes a longer period, the corrective wave is shorter and more abrupt.

The tenet or guiding principle of the theory is that an impulse wave is divided into five smaller waves whereas a corrective wave is divided into 3 impulse waves. A bull market therefore unfolds itself in five waves and a bear market in 3 but in directions opposite to one another.

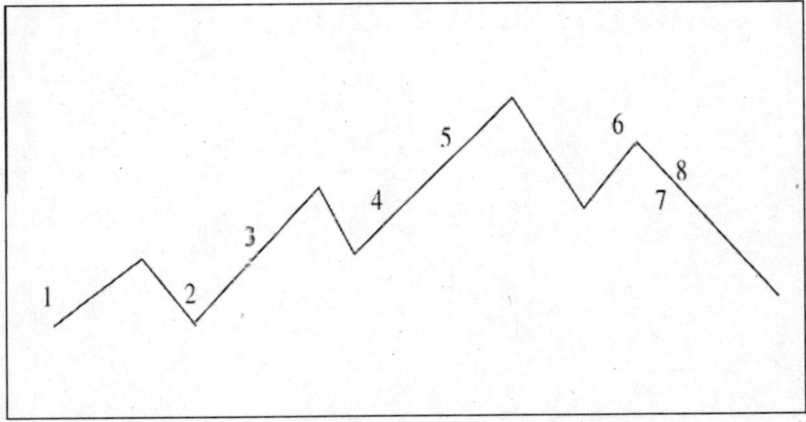

Figure 29.2: Now impulse waves and corrective waves complete a cycle.

In Figure 29.2, waves 1, 3 and 5 impulse waves are in the up direction. Wave 2 (correction of wave 1) and wave 4 (correction of wave 3) are in the down direction. These five waves constitute an impulse wave. This impulse wave is corrected by the next 3 waves 6 to 8. Here waves 6 and 8 are in the down direction and wave 7 is the corrective wave of wave 6. The 3 waves complete the corrective action and a cycle is completed. The market is now ready for the next impulse move.

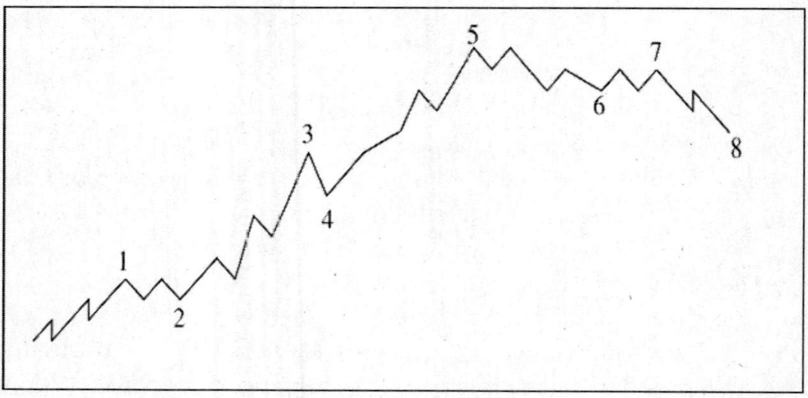

Figure 29.3

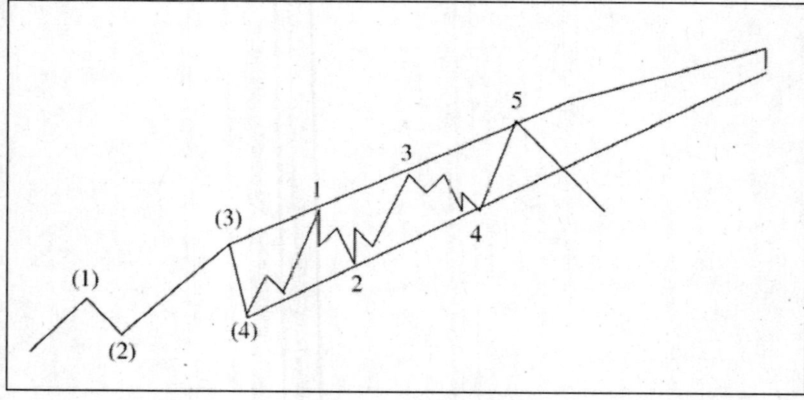

Figure 29.4

Detailed Classification of Waves

While studying trends using this theory, the main thing one needs to be able to do is to know when a wave ends and when the next starts. There can be small movements and corrections which occur but do not signify a wave. It would be noticed in Figure 29.3 that there are several movements within the main waves.

It is for this reason that, Elliot classified waves on the basis of their duration and extent (Table 29.1).

Table 29.1
Classification of Waves

Cycle	Period		
Grand Super Cycle	100	–	150 Years
Super Cycle	25	–	35 Years
Cycle	4	–	7 Years
Primary	6	–	15 Years
Intermediate	2	–	5 months
Minor or Sub wave	2	–	6 months
Minute	5	–	10 days
Minuette	8	–	10 hours
Sub-minuette	1	–	4 hours

The movement of the smallest minute wave in fives will constitute a wave of one degree higher in magnitude. Five minor waves will go on to form an intermediate wave and five intermediate waves will form a primary wave. Five primary waves will form a cycle wave and five cycle waves will form a super cycle (Figure 29.4).

Impulse waves are normally easier to follow as any two of them would normally be equal. If this is not so, then their relation would be close to 62%. This is based on Fibonacci's submissions and is known as the golden rule. Any one of these could become an extension when the market breaks new ground. When markets are very volatile, speculation is rife and there is general optimism. These are termed as "exaggerated movements" and will appear in one of the 3 impulse waves. The wave count in exaggerations will be in nines as opposed to fives. In such nine-wave situations, it is often difficult to identify the wave that is extended. It does not matter though as a wave of nine and a wave of five under this principle have the same technical implications.

Elliot Wave Theory maintains that only one of the three impulse waves would be extended. The extension is usually in the third or fifth impulse waves. The first wave is rarely extended. There are some other rules or characteristics of extension:

1. Extensions occur only in the new territory of the current cycle as they cannot occur anywhere else.
2. Extensions, if they occur in the fifth impulse wave, can be retraced twice.
3. An extension is never at the end of the movement.
4. The two non-extended waves are related to one another by the ratio of the Fibonacci numbers 1, 0.618 and 0.38 (Table 29.2).

Table 29.2

Numbers of Waves in One Complete Cycle

	Complete Bull Move	Complete Bear Move	Complete Cycle
Cyclical Waves	1	1	2
Primary Waves	5	3	8
Intermediate Waves	21	13	34
Minor Waves	89	55	144

A Word on Fibonacci

It is appropriate at this stage to discuss Fibonacci. Leonardo Fibonacci of Pisa was a mathematician who after extensive travels through Egypt presented to the world a sequence of numbers which is named after him. He maintained that each number is related to its previous number in the ratio of 1.618, e.g. 89 divided by 55 = 1.618. Each number is also related to the next Fibonacci number as 0.618, e.g. 89 divided by 144 = 0.618. Any number would have this relationship and called this Nature's Law of Growth.

Elliot maintained that Fibonacci's findings were relevant in the share market. When the market goes by 100 points, correction would bring it down by 0.618 or 0.382 (62% or 38%). Even rises can be correlated to Fibonacci's ratios. The best results are obtained when applied to the market averages as they are broad based. Distortions can occur in individual scrips.

On this basis, several pointers have emerged which can be useful in the forecasting trends. These include:

1. Diagonal triangles suggest the end of the ongoing move and precede a reversal.
2. Each of the five impulse waves and three corrective waves have characteristics of their own. This assists their classification.
3. For intermediate and large waves, advance or decline should be measured in percentage points.
4. Time sequence is maintained and exists.
5. The market follows the rule of alternation, i.e. alternate patterns, in virtually all wave movements. In a five-wave move, if the second is down zig zag, the fourth wave will be a triangle of sevens or elevens but not zig zag.
6. A price objective can be established at the beginning of the wave itself by channeling the wave.
7. The fifth wave is the Fibonacci's ratio of the net rise from the beginning of wave 1 to the end of wave 3.
8. Waves 6 and 8 are related as either 1 or 1.618.
9. The fourth wave in a 5-wave sequence should not overlap except within a diagonal triangle.

Like any other market theory, the Elliot Wave Theory must not be taken as gospel. There are times when movements don't take place as postulated. However, the theory is a guide to predicting market movement and if taken as such can be very rewarding.

~

Chapter 30

~

Trend Analysis

Trends of the prices of shares can be plotted to determine whether a share is on an uptrend or on a downtrend. These trend plottings are useful in determining whether one should purchase or sell a share.

So, how does it work?

In a bullish period, when prices are rising, the price trend will be similar to the illustration in Figure 30.1.

The price dips and rises but the trend is ascending. These uptrend lines connect two or more interim low prices with a straight line.

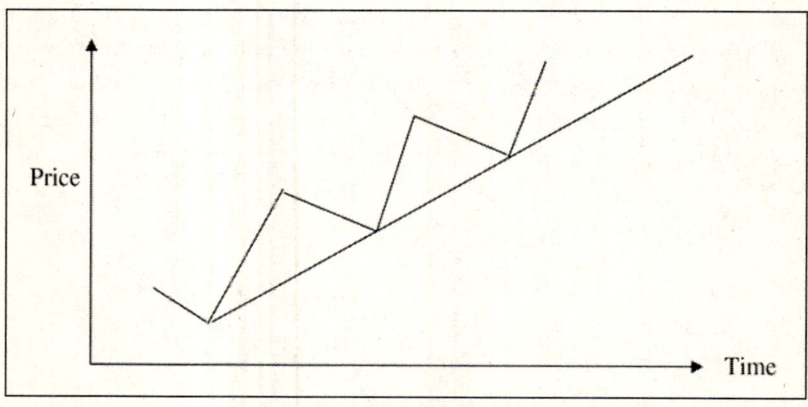

Figure 30.1: **A price uptrend**

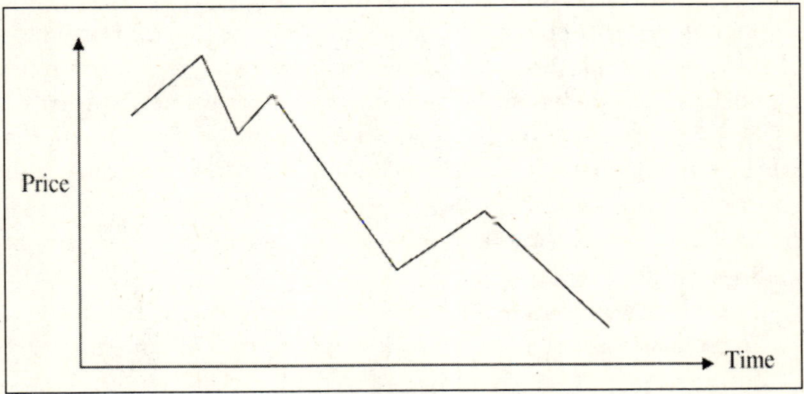

Figure 30.2: A price downtrend

On the other hand, in a bearish phase the price trend will show a definite decline. A downtrend line connects two or more peaks in a downward direction (Figure 30.2).

The secondary movements which reverse the direction of an uptrend are called reactions and movements that reverse the direction of a downtrend are called rallies.

There may be situations when although prices may rise, they return to their original price. These are known as horizontal trend lines (Figure 30.3).

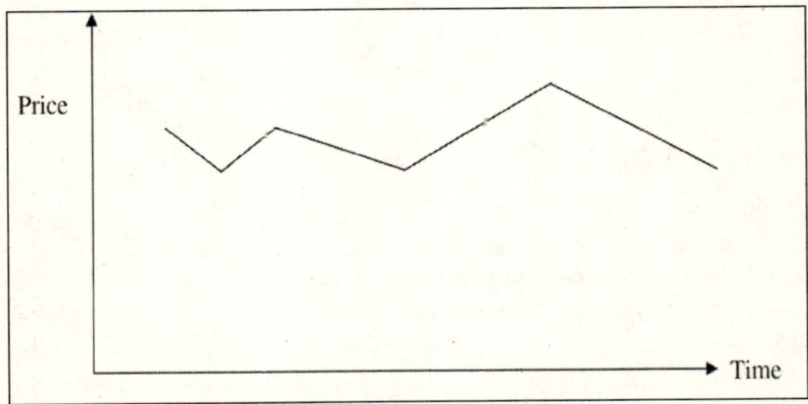

Figure 30.3: A horizontal trend line

If share prices follow a particular direction for a period of time, a channel gets established. A channel requires two trend lines drawn parallel to each other on either side of the price line. Normally a share price stays within its channel. The Dow Theory holds that when a trend starts, it tends to continue and does not change its course for some time. Thus, prices are expected to stay below down-trend lines, and *vice versa.* Additionally, these lines define support and resistance levels.

If trend lines are broken, it is assumed a new trend has started.

Trend lines are very useful in making decisions:

1. They indicate the trend of share prices. Thus, shares should only be bought when there is an uptrend.
2. Trend lines suggest when a share should be bought or sold. An investor who holds a share would tell another to sell just below an uptrend line. Similarly, he would buy when shares break upward from a downtrend line.

However, although they give indications, trend lines are not absolute guides and should not be taken as gospel. There could be other forces that might confuse trends. A trend line should be taken for what it is — an indication and not a certainty. As an investor or analyst, what one should try and identify is a change in trend. This is what will enable one to make a decision.

The general price patterns that emerge have been named as detailed below.

Price Patterns

Head and Shoulder

This pattern occurs when there are three successive rallies and reactions with the second one reaching the highest point, namely the "head" or "top," while the lowest point is the "shoulders" position. The shape emerges after an advance for a few weeks or some months. The left shoulder forms with the rising volume when the price rises and declines when the price falls. After this a second advance creates the head and then on the third rise the right shoulder is created. At each rally, the price touches the neckline before moving in the opposite direction.

If the right shoulder breaks through the neckline on the decline, it is interpreted as a signal to sell. A reverse head and shoulders pattern is interpreted to be bullish. There are several variations of this theme but this is the general principle.

Double Tops and Bottoms

In this scenario, the left peak is higher than the right. Volume is high on the first peak but drops in a marked manner when the second peak forms indicating that the bull that has no strength left. It is completed when, after the second top, the price falls below the valley between the peaks. This suggests the bull phase is over and bears begin to sell.

A double bottom is the opposite of the double top and signifies a buying opportunity. Of course, there could be triple tops and bottoms but these are not very common.

Support and Resistance Levels

At a support level there is sufficient demand to halt a fall in prices. This occurs when investors, believing the prices have fallen low enough, begin to purchase shares thus preventing further fall in prices.

Resistance levels, on the other hand, are where the rise in share prices is stopped. Shares are sold and the upward trend is stopped. This occurs when investors feel that the price has reached as high a level as it is likely to reach and begin to sell.

Speed Resistance Lines

This theory submits that the share price or the price index being measured will remain at a two-third speed resistance on a downward fall and reach the one-third resistance line. The one-third line should hold. If the one-third also fails, it suggests a new trend and that share prices would continue to fall. To calculate this, the two-thirds would be two-thirds of the increase from the last valley to the peak, from the initial price.

Gaps

Often, the opening price of a share on a particular day is either more or less than that of the closing price of the earlier day. This difference is known as the gap and occurs because of happenings between the last closing and the opening. There are several different types of gaps:

1. The breakaway gap occurs when a share breaks out of a horizontal price pattern with a gap.
2. A runaway gap happens by an extended price move happening in the same direction of the price move. Suppose a share has risen from ₹ 68 to ₹ 70 to ₹ 72 and then when it opens at ₹ 74, it would be termed as runaway gap.
3. An exhaustion gap is exactly the opposite of a runaway gap. A price may be going in a particular direction for some time and then may reverse in a different direction. The shares of a company may have been closing for a time at ₹ 68, ₹ 70, ₹ 72 and ₹ 74. If on the 5th day it opens at ₹ 71, the difference would be known as an exhaustion gap.
4. As island reversal occurs when prices gap in one direction and trade away from the gap. This is believed to signal an extended price move in the direction of the second gap.

Technical analysts maintain that most gaps will close. This will happen when the share trades inside the price range constituting the gap. If the hypothesis is accepted, the price would reverse and cover the area of the gap. If they accept this, investors can buy or sell (depending on the gap and the trend) to their profit.

Breakouts

Breakouts occur when prices break through a resistance level which would have earlier depressed the market with sellers selling shares. When this occurs, the demand exceeds supply and prices begin to rise. If volumes also increase, then prices will begin soaring. However, one must be careful before one begins buying at a breakout because it could be relatively short and one may find that he has bought the shares at a very high price.

Moving Averages

A moving average is the average of the closing prices of a share or index for the preceding few days. For example, a 7-day average will be as shown in Table 30.1.

Table 30.1

Calculating a 7-day moving average

Day	Price	Moving Average
1	58	
2	58	
3	58	
4	59	
5	59	
6	59	
7	60	58.71
8	62	59.29
9	62	59.86
10	63	60.59
11	64	61.29
12	65	62.14
13	68	63.43
14	70	64.86
15	70	66.00
16	68	66.85
17	66	67.29
19	64	67.29
20	62	66.86

The moving average is calculated from the 7th day taking into the account the average closing price of the previous seven days.

How to use moving average for trading and investing:

- When the moving average line cuts the actual price line from above, that is the time to buy share.
- When the moving average line cuts the actual price line from below, it is a sign to sell the shares.

Moving averages are useful in smoothing irregularities.

There are several other methods of determining price trends as such as:

1. The disparity index which compares the trends of two different groups of shares.
2. The absolute breadth indicator which measures the number of advancing shares as a per cent of the total number of shares.

3. The group diffusion index which compares the advances over a large number of industry groups.
4. The advance decline line which is a running total of the difference between the daily advances and declines.
5. Oscillators (overbought and oversold) which are calculated by dividing the number of advancing shares by the number of declines.

Charting

Charting is helpful for several reasons:

1. The trends help to forecast the direction share prices are likely to take and help one to make decisions.
2. They give one an insight to the thinking of the crowd.
3. Charting helps one to buy or sell shares before the general investing public.

Like other market tools, charting too is not foolproof. Charts and trends are an aid and should be treated as such. One should be careful not to use too many trend indicators because that can be very confusing — some may show an uptrend; others may show a downtrend and the result would leave one totally confused. I would recommend that before one acts, one should see whether the trend shown agrees with one's own assessment of the direction the prices are moving.

~

Chapter 31

~

Portfolio Management

Shares are not purchased with the sole intention of selling them promptly at a profit. They are assets that yield a return both in income and in capital appreciation and consequently are assets that can be used for savings and to enhance one's net worth. Additionally, as one saves, the savings need to be parked somewhere profitably. There is a limit to the number of houses or apartments one can buy. Fixed deposits with banks or other institutions are not particularly remunerative. Shares, on the other hand, appreciate at a rate exceeding the rate of inflation — often many times more. Also, one's share investment, especially in good blue chip companies, is fairly safe. Earlier these blue chip companies were controlled by the Tatas and Birlas — large business houses — or multinationals. The suggestion now is to look at the NIFTY 50 as the safest shares as they are reputed companies and large. These companies reward shareholders consistently though conservatively.

Anyone who purchases shares will, in time, end up with a portfolio. One may have a 100 shares each in 300 companies or just 5,000 shares each in 5 companies or just 200 shares each in 10 companies. The value of one's portfolio may be ₹ 10,000 or ₹ 1,00,000 or ₹ 10,00,000 or even ₹ 1,00,00,000. Irrespective of whether the portfolio is small or large, it must be managed if it is to grow effectively. It must be fit and lean, with no fat. The weeds must be taken out periodically. Otherwise, the growth in the portfolio's value would be sluggish and its yield less than satisfactory. Hence, it is important that one should properly manage one's portfolio in order to maximize returns.

Portfolio Size

The shares one chooses to buy would always be based on one's natural bent. If one is conservative blue chips would be purchased and held for a long period of time. On the other hand, the speculative investor would purchase volatile shares in the hope of a quick profit. Be that as it may, it is important to limit the number of companies whose shares one has. The reason for this is simple. It is not possible to keep track of more than a few companies at a time. If one has shares in 400 companies, it will be incredibly difficult to keep track of company results, dividend payments, etc., unless of course one is a professional investment manager. Even then it would take up a ridiculously long period of time. The average investor does not have such time. At best — and I am stating this after having spoken to a cross-section of investors —, the investor has a hurried 45 minutes in the morning and an hour in the evening. In this time it is not possible to keep abreast of the happenings of and information on more than 20 to 25 companies, if that.

How many companies should you invest in? What should be the size of your portfolio? To answer this question you should determine how many companies you can review periodically. If you believe you can review 40 companies, then you should invest in not more than 40 companies. If, on the other hand, you feel that you can review only 20 companies, then you should not invest in more than 20 companies. The point is, you should be clear on how many companies you can meaningfully review and you should not hold shares in more than that. This also means never exceeding the limit that you've set yourself. Let us assume you feel you can review 25 companies and you hold shares in 25 companies. If you buy shares of yet another company, it is imperative that you sell the shares of a company that you hold in order to get back to your 25 figure. By doing this one will control one's portfolio and be able to give each investment personalized attention. You will know which company is doing well and which company is not. If a company is doing badly you will be able to get rid of it before the price crashes and if a company is doing well you well watch to purchase more shares. Thus, as an investor, you will be forever ahead.

Investment / Share Review

It is important to review your investments regularly. Failure to do so can lead to losses.

In reviewing your investments you should check the performance of your shares against a target that you have set and its performance within the industry or the market average. This review should be done at least once a quarter and after the review shares that have not performed should be sold and new targets should be laid down.

It must, however, be remembered that it may not be prudent in certain conditions to sell your investments just because targets laid down have not been met in one quarter. If you reviewed targets set in May 2006 (when the market crashed) you may have ended up selling all your shares. That would have been both inappropriate and unwise. One must review performance realistically taking into account the political and economic environment. A chart for a quarterly review is detailed in Table 31.1.

Table 31.1

Quarterly Portfolio Review

Sl. No.	Name of share	Price on 1 Oct.	Target 31 Dec.	Market Price 31 Dec.	Increase / Decrease %	Industry Increase / Decrease	Decision
1	Bombay Cotton	125	160	160	28	30	Retain
2	Warden Tubes	78	180	31	100	100	Buy More
3	Samudra Fisheries	210	275	240	14	12	Sell
4	Ruby Diamonds	38	50	44	16	20	Sell
5	Anand Sports	12	16	24	100	95	Buy more

Apart from a quarterly chart one should also review investments on a daily basis. This will give one an opportunity to be familiar with price movement over a period of time and will enable one to take prompt buy or sell action.

Such a daily review will not take much time. After determining what the closing prices were, these should be written down preferably on columnar paper. If possible, the prices should also be plotted on graph paper. This will give a physical representation of prices over a period of time and can assist one in evolving an investment strategy. Graphs can be improved by superimposing monthly average prices of the shares and the daily highs and lows. This does not now require much work as such computerised charts are easily available on the internet, etc.

Set Targets

Shares are not held for sentimental reasons. They are held for income and for profit. Consequently on purchasing a share, you, should set a price target for each share. The target will naturally vary according to the type of share purchased. If the share is speculative, the targeted growth or expectation may be as high as 50%. On the other hand, if it is a conservative share you may target a growth of only 10%. The target should be for a specific period of time — 3 months, 6 months or a year, and performance must be examined at the end of that period. As was stated in the earlier section, if the target has not been met or if the possibility exists of it not being met the share should be sold. On the other hand, if the target has been met, a decision should be taken whether to continue holding it or not. If the decision is to hold the share, then new targets should be set.

While reviewing performance against targets consideration must be made for extremes. In a bull phase shares may double whereas in a bear phase the opposite may happen. Therefore, some adjustment should be made for such happenings.

Shun Sentimentality

Sentimentality has no place in investments. A share is purchased for the gains one anticipates or the income it is likely to generate. A purchase of a share must never be considered as an acquisition for life, it's not a matter of "to love and to cherish till death do us part." As soon as a share has outlived its usefulness, or served the purpose

Illustration 31.1

Ajay made his first investment in shares in 1990 by purchasing 500 shares of Vijay Limited. Over the years he has bought and sold many shares but for sentimental reasons he has not parted with this first purchase of his. His original cost was ₹ 40 per share. Initially, the company had regularly paid dividends of 20% and had issued a bonus of 1 share for every 1 held. It was quoted in 2005 as high as ₹ 110 a share. However, the industry then fell on hard times. The management had by then become top heavy and complacent. Overheads were very high. The quality of the products deteriorated and the company lost its market share. In September 2015, the shares were quoted at ₹ 35 per share. The appreciation in 25 years was only ₹ 15,000, which was less than 3% per year. In reality, if one considers inflation, the value of the investment has actually fallen. Ajay suffered this as he held onto the particular share because it represented his first investment.

Ajay could have done a number of things:

- In 2005, he could have sold 200 shares thereby realizing his original investment.
- In 2005, he could have also sold 500 shares thus making a good profit on his investment and still retained his original 500 shares which would, in effect, have cost him nothing.
- In 2005 he could have sold his entire holding, realized a tremendous profit and then used the proceeds to invest in the shares of another company that had good growth prospects

To his detriment, Ajay chose to superstitiously and sentimentally hang onto the shares. In my opinion, if he had to be sentimental, then as opposed to holding onto 1,000 shares as Ajay did (original 500 plus bonus 500), he should have held on onto only 100 shares and sold the rest. He would have thus reaped enormous profits and yet satisfied his sentimental desire of holding onto a portion of this first investment.

for which it was purchased it should be sold off. If one holds onto it indefinitely, it could result in a loss. Times change, returns could be less and eventually when one wants to sell the share, it may be too late (*see* Illustration 31.1).

Stay Well Informed

It is imperative that one is aware of happenings in the economy, in the industry a company one has invested in, and in the company itself because these can make the share soar to Olympian heights or plunge to Hadic depths. Duties may have increased or decreased; interest rates may have been increased; a liberalized policy may have been announced; the dynamic managing director may have died; the controlling family may be squabbling, and the likes — all these have an impact on share prices. The European crisis in 2015 resulted in share prices plunging. The election in 2014 of Narendra Modi and the Bharatiya Janata Party resulted in sahares booming. A mention by the Finance Minister in December 2015 that banks must pass on the interest rate cuts to customers led to a decline in bank share prices. The investor must be aware and must take prompt corrective action. Otherwise, he stands to lose substantially. Correspondingly, by staying well informed, he stands to make a killing, too. In short one should keep one's eyes and ears open.

Diversify Your Portfolio

A diversified portfolio ensures that one is cushioned against a downturn in an industry. It is very risky placing all one's money in one company or in one industry since a downturn can wipe out the value of the portfolio.

In short, by diversifying one's portfolio one is able to hedge industry recession. It is rare for all industries to be doing badly at the same time. The shares held in one company may go down on account of various factors but then the shares held in others may increase in price — thus neutralizing the effect of a slump in an industry.

It must be realized that it need not only be a slump in an industry that beats shares prices down. There could be other extraneous factors such as a large tax demand.

One should, therefore, not invest in just one company or industry. The question that logically arises then is how much can be invested. There is no hard and fast dictum on this — it will depend on one's ability to take risk, one's nature and the like. As a thumb rule in my personal opinion one should:

1. Limit one's investment in any single industry to around 15%.
2. Limit one's investment in a single company to 10%.

This will ensure a reasonable spread.

Don't Fall in Love with Your Shares

A share is a commodity that one buys for gain — gain in the form of income and capital appreciation and it should be treated exactly like that. One should not fall in love with a share and hold it because the name is melodious or the chairman is a celebrity. These are wrong reasons for holdings a share and will lead only to unhappiness and losses.

Control Your Avarice

"No matter how fast you are there is always someone faster than you." This was a saying among gunfighters in the Wild West who were perennially trying to prove their mettle by constantly challenging others to a duel and often dying in gunfights due to an overestimation of their caliber.

This can quite successfully be adapted to the stock market too. It is well nigh impossible to always buy at the bottom of the market and to sell at the top. No one can do it. It is best to buy at relatively low price and sell at a time when the share is rising.

Usually when a share is rising one holds on in the belief that it would continue to rise and that one will make a fortune. He usually does not know nor has he considered what the peak would be. He holds onto the share and his beliefs. The share usually peaks and then declines and the optimistic shareholder feels aggrieved at a reversal without even once admitting that perhaps he was being greedy.

Similarly, in a bear market when one finds shares falling in price, one does not purchase in the belief that the market has not fallen fully and that one would, be later able to pick up the share for the proverbial song. On such themes are legends written. It doesn't usually happen. The share prices after hitting a low will begin to rise and no longer remains a paying proposition.

One cannot wait for the market price to reach the absolute zenith to sell, or for it to reach rock bottom to buy. These decisions should be taken when the share price has reached a level at which the likelihood exists of the individual making a reasonable return.

As a rule of thumb, it is reasonable and logical to begin selling shares once the price has increased by 20% of one's purchase price and then to progressively sell as prices go up. Similarly it is a good idea to buy when the price falls by 30% to 40% below the peak price the shares had reached unless there are some mitigating reasons (*see* Illustration 31.2).

Illustration 31.2

Rampole Hindustan Ltd. is a company engaged in the manufacture of fans. It has been a steady, dividend paying company.

Rampole's shares were on 1 July 2015 quoted at ₹ 22. The highest and lowest price it had reached in 2015 was ₹ 29 and ₹ 18 respectively. As soon as the share reaches ₹ 25 the shareholder should sell atleast 20% holding and book profits. If it rises again, he should dispose of some more If he sits and waits for it to rise to ₹ 35 or so, it may never do so. Similarly, at ₹ 22 it may be worth purchasing. The share may fall further but it may not. It has, on the other hand, demonstrated that it actually can go upto ₹ 29 suggesting that there is a short term chance (should the price go up) of making a clean profit of over 30%.

Cut Your Losses – Fast

One purchases shares to make money or to receive income or as a hedge against inflation or for some other similar reason. As an investment, shares must be closely watched and if there is a possibility (however remote that may be) that prices are likely to fall and keep on falling, it will be proper to sell them immediately even if it is at a loss. This is to save oneself from a greater loss at a future time (*see* Illustration 31.3).

Illustration 31.3

Shyam, a friend of mine, purchased a 100 shares of XYZ Industries in 2015 at the then ruling price of ₹ 36 per share. The company had a good reputation at that time. The prices then began to plunge because the company began to go through a terrible period. There was a depression in the industry and the company was unable to sell its goods. Shyam did not sell. The price fell to ₹ 19 per share. Shyam held on. The price fell again and again. Shyam did not want to book a loss and so he held on. Six years later the company was on its knees. Shyam then found that there were no takers for the shares though he was now prepared to sell the share at any price – ₹ 4 per share, ₹ 3 per share – anything. But no one wanted them.

Book Your Profits

Until you have actually booked your profits, you have not made a profit. Paper profits are meaningless. They are here today and gone tomorrow. The question that really arises is — what should one do? As a general rule — irrespective of the price the share will subsequently attain — one should sell 20% of one's holding as soon as the price reaches 20% above his purchased price. He should offload another 30% when the price reaches 40% above his purchase price. In this way he reduces his take and maintains an interest.

"A bird in hand is worth two in the bush."

A friend of mine in early 2015 bought 1,000 shares of XYZ Ltd. at ₹ 219 per share. The price rose rapidly to ₹ 423. My friend patted himself on being a tremendous picker of shares. On an investment of ₹ 19,000 he had in a few months made a profit of nearly 60%. But he did nothing about it. The market worsened. Orders ceased and the company collapsed. I have now a sad friend who has not fully recovered from the episode. What should he have done? He should have, when the price reached ₹ 423 offloaded the shares (*see* Illustration 31.4).

Illustration 31.4

Mr. Sharma purchased 1,000 shares of Expandex Ltd. at ₹ 20 per share on 5 January 2015.

On 2 March 2015 the price was ₹ 24.50 per share.

At this price he sold 200 shares

On 23 May 2015 the price was ₹ 28 per share. At this price he sold 300 shares.

The position on 1 June 2015 would be:

	₹
5 January 2015 purchase of 1,000 shares	20,000
2 March 2015 sale of 200 shares	4,900
	15,100
23 May 2015 sale of 300 shares	8,400
	₹ 6,700

The value of 500 shares is now ₹ 6,700 or ₹ 13.40 a share which is a much reduced price from the original ₹ 20 per share.

On 18 June 2015 the price reached ₹ 31 per share. Mr. Sharma sold a further 200 shares and received a cheque for ₹ 6,200.

Contd...

Illustration 31.4 *(... contd)*

His investment now in 300 shares of Expandex Ltd. is only ₹ 500, the cost being ₹ 1.66 per share – a far cry from his original cost of ₹ 20 per share. Now Mr. Sharma cannot lose, whatever happens.

In short, it is important to slowly book profits whenever prices rise so that one's stake is reduced. If prices fall, one can always buy into the share again at a future date. As Meyer Rothschild once said "You never go broke by taking a profit."

~

Chapter 32

~

Taxation

"Taxes are what we pay for a civilized society."

— Oliver Wendell Holmes Jr.

Taxation is an important factor in investment planning because the objective of investment for growth or income is to maximize the net returns which is, in effect the after tax returns.

The manner one is exposed to taxation is on the income one earns on shares in the form of dividends and on the profit one makes when he sells shares. In addition, one may receive a benefit in kind, like bonus shares, or there may be stock splits or buybacks.

Dividends

Dividends received are not taxable in the hands of individuals.

Gain on the Sale of Shares

Gains on shares held for a year or more are not taxable as these are considered long term gains.

Shares held for less than a year are considered short term gains. Any short term losses suffered can be set off against these gains. The net gain is taxed at 10%.

Bonus Shares

Bonus shares are issued to investors by capitalizing reserves. They are issued in proportion to the holding an investor has in the company. If a company issues a 1:1 bonus issue, an investor will get one additional share for every share he holds in the company. This does not change the ownership pattern — it merely increases the number of shares in circulation.

After the bonus issue, as the number of shares increase, the price per share will fall to take into account the increased number of shares.

Bonus issues are perceived as a strong signal that the company is doing well and is investor friendly. It is an indicator that the management believes the company's profits are likely to increase. The belief is that the management would not have issued bonus shares if it was not confident of distributing dividends on all the shares in the future.

Since no money is paid to acquire bonus shares, bonus shares are not valued at "nil cost" for tax purposes.

Stock Splits

Stock splits are becoming increasingly popular in India. With an increase in the price of shares, companies are beginning to split their stock. This effectively means that they reduce the face value of the share. Recently, for example, the ₹ 10 shares of Indian Hotels were trading at between ₹ 1,350 and ₹ 1,400 per share. The company split the ₹ 10 share to 10 shares of ₹ 1 each. These then began to be traded at around ₹ 145. The intent was to make the share appear more affordable and infuse more liquidity. Most big companies have resorted to splits from time to time including ITC, Infosys, Blue Star, Satyam, etc.

It should be remembered that in a stock split, the capital of the company remains the same whereas in a bonus issue, the capital increases and the reserves fall. However, like in bonus issues, the company's net worth (capital + reserves) is not affected.

There are no tax implications of a stock split for the investor. If the share has been bought at ₹ 1,400 and a 10 for 1 split has occurred, the share would be assumed to have been bought at ₹ 140.

Share Buybacks

Share buybacks are becoming common. Companies such as Siemens, Infosys and Reliance have bought back their shares.

By buying back shares, a corporate gets flexibility. It enables a company to sustain a higher debt-equity ratio and can be effective in warding off hostile takeovers. Companies buy their shares back when they feel their shares are undervalued, or when they have excess cash. It also prevents dilution of earnings.

With regard to buyback, it should be determined whether the amount paid is a dividend or a consideration for transfer of shares. If it is considered dividend, it is not taxable. The question would arise too as to what is the dividend — the entire amount or the amount above the face value of the share.

It has been held that where any company purchases its own shares, the difference between the consideration received by the shareholder and the cost of acquisition will be deemed to be capital gains. Further, it will not be treated as dividends as the definition of dividend does not include payments made by a company to purchases its own shares.

~

Chapter 33

~

Annual Report

The primary and most important source of information about a company is its Annual Report. By law, this is prepared every year and distributed to the shareholders.

Annual reports are usually very well presented. A tremendous amount of data is given about the performance of a company over a period of time. Multi-coloured pie and bar charts are included to illustrate and explain to the shareholders facts such as the growth of the company and the manner in which the revenue earned has been utilized. There are pictures of the newly painted factory; of new machines acquired, of the chairman at his desk looking forbidding yet wise and of the board of directors — the directors individually attempting to appear professional, capable and yet benevolent. As a consequence annual reports tend to be bulky.

The average shareholder does not look much further. If the Annual Report appears worthy of the company whose name it bears, if the photographs are impressive and the company has paid a reasonable dividend, the typical shareholder reads no more. He sits back content in the belief that the fortunes of the company are in good hands.

This must not be the criteria by which a company is judged. Rather than be convinced on the state of the affairs of a company by gazing at charts and impressive arrays of figures and statistics, the reader of the report, whether he be investor or shareholder or creditor or just another interested person would be wise to delve deeper to read between and beyond the lines and to peep behind the figures.

The annual report is broken down into the following specific parts:

1. The Director's Report,
2. The Auditor's Report,
3. The Financial Statements, and
4. The Schedules and Notes to the Accounts.

Each of these parts has a purpose and a tale to tell. The tale should be heard.

The Directors' Report

The Directors' Report is a report submitted by the directors of a company to its shareholders, advising them of the performance of the company under their stewardship. It is, in effect, the report they submit to justify their continued existence and it is because of this that these reports should be read with a pinch of salt. After all, if a group of individuals have to present an evaluation of their own performance, they are bound to highlight their achievements and gloss over their failures. It is natural. It is human nature. Consequently, all these reports are very well written. Every sentence, nay every word, is subjected to the most piercing scrutiny. Every happening of importance is catalogued and highlighted to convince a casual reader that the company is in good hands. And there is a tendency to justify unhappy happenings. Nevertheless, the a directors' report provides an investor valuable information:

1. It enunciates the opinion of the directors on the state of the economy and the political situation *vis-à-vis* the company.
2. It explains the performance and the financial results of the company in the period under review. This is an extremely important part. The results and operations of the various separate divisions are usually detailed and investors can determine the reasons for their good or bad performance.
3. The Directors' Report details the company's plans for modernization, expansion and diversification. Without these, a company will remain static and eventually decline.
4. It discusses the profit earned in the period under review and the dividend recommended by the directors. This paragraph should

normally be read with some skepticism, as the directors will always argue that the performance was satisfactory. If profits have improved it would invariably be because of superior marketing and hard work in the face of severe competition. If low, adverse economic conditions are usually at fault.

5. It elaborates on the directors' views of the company's prospects in the future.
6. It discusses plans for new acquisition and investments.

An investor must intelligently evaluate the issues raised in a directors' report. Diversification is good but does it make sense? Industry conditions and the management's knowledge of the business must be considered. A diversification that was a disaster was United Breweries' diversification into airlines (Kingfisher). So was Metal Box's move into ball bearings and Spartek's acquisition of Neycer Ceramics. The point I am trying to make is that although companies must diversify in order to spread the risks of industrial slumps, every diversification may not suit a company. Similarly, all other issues raised in the directors' report should be analyzed. Did the company perform as well as others in the same industry? Is the finance being raised the most logical and beneficial for the company? It is imperative that the investor read between the lines of a directors' report and find the answers to these questions.

In short, a directors' report is valuable and if read intelligently can give the investor a good grasp of the workings of a company, the problems it faces, the direction it intends taking, and its future prospects.

The Auditor's Report

The auditor represents the shareholders and it is his duty to report to the shareholders and the general public on the stewardship of the company by its directors. Auditors are required to report whether the financial statements presented do, in fact, present a true and fair view of the state of the company. Investors must remember that the auditors are their representatives and that they are required by law to point out if the financial statements are not true and fair. They are also required to report any change, such as a change in accounting principles or the non-provision of charges that result in an undue increase or reduction in profits. It is really the only impartial report that a shareholder or investor receives and this alone should spur one to scrutinize the auditor's report minutely. Unfortunately, more often than not it is not read.

There can be interesting contradictions. It was stated in the Auditor's Report of a well known company that, "As at the year end 31st March 2015 the accumulated losses exceed the net worth of the Company and the Company has suffered cash losses in the financial year ended 31st March 2015 as well as in the immediately preceding financial year. In our opinion, therefore, the Company is a sick industrial company within the meaning of clause (O) of Section 3(1) of the Sick Industrial Companies (Special Provisions) Act 1985." The Directors' Report however stated, "The financial year under review has not been a favorable year for the Company as the Computer Industry in general continued to be in the grip of recession. High input costs as well as resource constraints hampered operations. The performance of your Company must be assessed in the light of these factors. During the year manufacturing operations were curtailed to achieve cost effectiveness. Your directors are confident that the efforts for increased business volumes and cost control will yield better results in the current year."

The auditors were of the opinion that the company was sick whereas the directors spoke optimistically of their hope that the future would be better! I suppose they could not, being directors, state otherwise.

When reading an auditor's report, the effect of their qualification may not be apparent. The auditor's report of another company stated: "In our opinion and to the best of our information and explanation given to us, the said accounts subject to Note 3 regarding doubtful debts, Note. 4 regarding balance confirmations, Note. 5 on custom liability and interests thereon, Note. 11 on product development expenses, Note. 14 on gratuity, Note 8 16(C) and 16(F) regarding stocks, give the information in the manner as required by the Companies Act 2013, and give a true and fair view."

Let us now look at the specific notes in this case:

1. Note 3 stated that no provision had been made for doubtful debts.

2. It was noted in Note 4 that balance confirmation of sundry debtors, sundry creditors and loans and advances had not been obtained.
3. It was stated in Note 5 that customs liability and interest thereon worth ₹ 3,14,30,073 against the imported raw materials lying in the ICF/Bonded godown had not been provided.
4. Note 11 drew attention to the fact that product development expenses worth ₹ 17,44,049 were being written off over ten years from 2009-2019. ₹ 2,16,51,023 had been capitalized under this head relating to the development of CT142, Digital TV, CFBT which shall be written off in 10 years.
5. The company's share towards past gratuity liabilities had neither been ascertained nor provided for except to the extent of premiums paid against an LIC group gratuity policy taken by the trust. (Note 14.)
6. Note 16C stated that the raw material consumed had been estimated by the management and this had not been checked by the auditors.

The company made a profit of just over ₹ 1 crore. If the product development expenses, customer duty and interest and provision for bad debts had been made as is required under generally accepted accounting principles, the profit would have turned into a loss.

The point to remember is that at times accounting principles are changed or creative and innovative accounting practices are resorted to by some companies in order to show a better result. The effect of these changes is at times not detailed in the notes to the accounts. The auditor's report will always draw the attention of the reader to these changes and the effect that these have on the financial statements. It is for this reason that a careful reading of the auditor's report is not only necessary but mandatory for an investor.

Financial Statements

The published financial statements of a company in an annual report consist of its Balance Sheet as at the end of the accounting period detailing the financial condition of the company at that date, and the Profit and Loss Account or Income Statement summarizing the activities of the company for the accounting period.

Pazirini Ltd.
Balance Sheet as at 31 March 2015

₹ in lakhs

	2014	2015
SOURCES OF FUNDS		
Shareholder's funds:		
(a) Capital	1,000	1,000
(b) Reserves	800	1,650
	1,800	2,650
Loan funds:		
(a) Secured Loans	1,350	1,050
(b) Unsecured Loans	650	500
	2,000	1,550
Total	3,800	4,200
APPLICATION OF FUNDS		
Fixed Assets	3,200	3,640
Investments	400	400
Current Assets :		
Trade Debtors	600	700
Prepaid Expenses	80	80
Cash & Bank Balances	50	100
Other Current Assets	100	150
	830	1,030
Less:		
Current Liabilities and Provisions:		
Trade Creditors	480	710
Accrued Expenses	70	90
Sundry Creditors	80	70
	630	870
Net Current Assets	200	160
Total	3,800	4,200

Pazirini Ltd.
Profit & Loss Account for the year ended 31 March 2015

₹ in lakhs

	2014	2015
INCOME		
Sales	14,000	17,500
Other income	500	600
	14,500	18,100
EXPENDITURE		
Materials	7,600	9,200
Employment	3,450	3,900
Operating & other expenses	1,150	2,100
Interest & finance charges	300	350
Depreciation	80	100
	12,580	15,650
Profit for the year before tax	1,920	2,450
Taxation	900	1,200
	1,020	1,250
APPROPRIATIONS		
Dividend	220	400
General reserves	200	400
	420	800
BALANCE CARRIED FORWARD	600	450

Balance Sheet

The balance sheet details the financial position of a company on a particular date; of the company's assets (that which the company owns), and liabilities (that which the company owes), grouped logically under specific heads. It must, however, be noted that the Balance Sheet details the financial position on a particular day and that the position can be materially different on the next day or the day after (*see* Illustration 33.1).

Illustration 33.1

Puniya Limited had taken a loan of ₹ 200 lakh on 1 December 2014 which was repayable on 1 April 2015. On 31 March 2015, its Balance Sheet was as follows:

Puniya Ltd.

Balance Sheet as at 31 March 2015

(In rupees lakh)

Shareholders' funds	100	Fixed assets	70
Loan funds	200	Investments	30
Current liabilities	20	Current assets	220
	320		320

Current assets include cash of ₹ 200 lakh to repay the loan. Puniya Ltd. did repay the loans, as promised on 1 April 2015. Its Balance Sheet after the repayment read:

Puniya Ltd.

Balance Sheet as at 1 April 2015

(In rupees lakh)

Shareholders funds	100	Fixed assets	70
Loan funds	-	Investments	30
Current liabilities	20	Current assets	20
	120		120

An investor reviewing the two balance sheets would be forgiven for drawing two very different conclusions. At 31 March 2015, Puniya Limited would be considered a highly leveraged company — one financed by borrowings. On 1 April 2015, on the other hand, it would be concluded that the company was very conservative and undercapitalized, as a consequence of which its growth would be limited.

Sources of Funds

A company has to source funds to purchase fixed assets, to procure working capital and to fund its business. For the company to make a profit, the funds have to cost less than the return the company earns on their deployment.

Where does a company raise funds? What are the sources?

Companies raise funds both as capital from its shareholders and as loans by borrowing.

Shareholders' Funds

A company sources funds from shareholders either by the issue of shares or by ploughing back profits. Shareholders' funds represent the stake they have in the company; the investment they have made.

SHARE CAPITAL

Share capital represents the shares issued by the company to the public. This is issued in following ways:

1. **Private placement:** This is done by offering shares to selected individuals or institutions.
2. **Public issue:** Shares are offered to the public. The details of the offer, including the reasons for raising the money are detailed in a prospectus and it is important that investors read this. Till the scam of 1992, public issues were extremely popular as the shares were often issued to investors at a price much lower than their real value. As a consequence, they were oversubscribed many times. This is no longer true. As companies are now free to price their issues as they like, and the office of the controller of capital issues has been abolished, companies typically price their shares at what the market can bear. This is done with the help of merchant bankers through a book building exercise. It is often well worth investing in good companies at the offer price, as prices have appreciated significantly on listing.
3. **Rights issues:** Companies may also issue shares to their shareholders as a matter of right in proportion to their holding. This was often done at a price lower than its market value and shareholders stood to gain enormously. With the new-found freedom in respect of pricing of shares, companies have begun pricing them nearer their intrinsic value. Consequently, these issues have not been particularly attractive to investors and several have failed to be fully subscribed.
4. **Bonus shares:** Bonus shares are shares issued free to shareholders by capitalizing reserves. No monies are actually raised from shareholders. It can be argued, however, that if these shares are issued by capitalizing distributable reserves, i.e. profits not distributed as dividends, then, in effect, shareholders are not being given anything.

RESERVES

Reserves are profits or gains which are retained in the companies and not distributed. Companies have two kinds of reserves — capital reserves and revenue reserves:

1. **Capital reserves:** Capital reserves are gains that have resulted from an increase in the value of assets and they are not freely distributable to the shareholders. The most of common capital reserves one comes across is the share premium account arising from the issue of shares at a premium, and the capital revaluation reserve, namely unrealized gain on the value of assets.
2. **Revenue reserves:** These represent profits from operations ploughed back into the company and not distributed as dividends to shareholders. It is important that all the profits are not distributed as funds are required by companies to purchase new assets to replace existing ones for expansion and for working capital.

Loan Funds

The other source of funds a company has access to are borrowings. Borrowing is often preferred by companies as it is quicker, relatively easier and the rules that need to be complied with are far fewer. The loans taken by companies are either:

SECURED LOANS

These loans are taken by a company by pledging some of its assets, or by a floating charge on some or all of its assets. The usual secured loans a company has are debentures and term loans.

UNSECURED LOAN

Companies do not pledge any assets when they take unsecured loans. The comfort a lender has is usually only the good name and credit worthiness of the company. The more common unsecured loans of a company are fixed deposits and short term loans. In case a company is dissolved, unsecured lenders are usually paid after the secured lenders have been satisfied.

Borrowings or credits for working capital which fluctuate such as bank overdrafts and trade creditors are not normally classified as loan funds but as current liabilities.

Application of Funds

Fixed assets

Fixed assets are assets that a company owns for use in its business and to produce goods. They are not for resale and typically comprises of land, buildings, i.e. offices, warehouses and factories, vehicles, machinery, furniture, equipment, and the like.

Every company has some fixed assets though the nature or kind of fixed assets vary from company to company. A manufacturing company's major fixed assets would be its factory and machinery, whereas that of a shipping company would be its ships.

Fixed assets are shown in the balance sheet at cost less the accumulated depreciation. Depreciation is based on the very sound concept that an asset has a useful life, and that after years of toil it wears down. Consequently, it attempts to measure that wear and tear and to reduce the value of the asset accordingly so that at the end of its useful life, the asset will have no value. As depreciation is a charge on profits, at the end of its useful life, the company would have set aside from profits an amount equal to the original cost of the asset and this could be utilized to purchase another asset. However, in these inflationary times, this is inadequate and some companies create an additional reserve to ensure that there are sufficient funds to replace worn out assets. The common methods of depreciation are:

1. **Straight line method:** The cost of the asset is written off equally over its life. Consequently, at the end of its useful life, the cost will equal the accumulated depreciation.
2. **Reducing balance:** Under this method depreciation is calculated on the written down value, namely cost less depreciation. Consequently, depreciation is higher in the beginning and lower since the years progress. An asset is never fully written off since the depreciation is always calculated on a reducing balance.
3. **Other Methods:** There are a few other methods, such as the interest method and the rule of 72 but these are not commonly used.

Land is the only fixed asset that is never depreciated as it normally appreciates in value. Capital work in progress — factories being constructed, etc. — is not depreciated until it is a fully functional asset.

Investments

Many companies purchase investments in the form of shares or debentures to earn income or to utilize cash surpluses profitably. The normal investments a company has are:

TRADE

Trade investments are shares or debentures of competitors that a company holds to have access to information on their growth, profitability and other details which may not otherwise, be easily available.

SUBSIDIARY AND ASSOCIATE COMPANIES

These are shares held in subsidiary or associate companies. The large business houses hold controlling interest in several companies through cross holdings in subsidiary and associate companies.

OTHERS

Companies also often hold shares or debentures of other companies for investment or to park surplus funds.

Investments are also classified as quoted and unquoted investments. Quoted investments are shares and debentures that are quoted on a recognized stock exchange and can be freely traded. Unquoted investments are not listed or quoted on any stock exchange. Consequently, these are not liquid and are difficult to dispose of.

Investments are valued and stated in the balance sheet at either the acquisition cost or market value, whichever is lower. This is in order to be conservative and to ensure that losses are adequately accounted for.

Current Assets

Current assets are assets owned by a company which are used in the normal course of business or are generated by the company in the course of business, such as debtors or finished stock or cash. The rule of thumb is that any asset that is turned into cash within twelve months is a current asset.

Current assets can be divided essentially into three categories:

1. **Converting assets:** Assets that are produced or generated in the normal course of business, such as finished goods and debtors.
2. **Constant assets:** Constant assets are those that are purchased and sold without any add-ons or conversions — liquor bought by a liquor store from liquor manufacturers.
3. **Cash equivalents:** They can be used to repay dues or purchase other assets. The most common cash equivalent assets are cash in hand and at the bank, and loans given.

The current assets a company has are:

STOCK OR INVENTORIES

These are arguably the most important current assets that a company has as it is by the sale of its stocks that a company makes its profits. Stocks, in turn, consist of:

1. **Raw materials:** The primary purchase which is utilized to manufacture the products a company makes.
2. **Work in progress:** Goods that are in the process of manufacture but are yet to be completed.
3. **Finished goods:** The finished products manufactured by the company that are ready for sale.

Stocks are valued at the lower of cost or net realizable value. This is to ensure that there will be no loss at the time of sale as that would have been accounted for.

The common methods of valuing stocks are:

1. **FIFO or first in first out:** It is assumed under this method that stocks that come in first would be sold first and those that come in last would be sold last.
2. **LIFO or last in first out:** The premise on which this method is based is the opposite of FIFO. It is assumed that the stocks that arrive last will be sold first. The reasoning is that customers prefer newer materials or products.

It is important to ascertain the method of valuation and the accounting principles involved as stock values can easily be manipulated by changing the method of valuation.

TRADE DEBTORS

Most companies do not sell their products for cash but on credit and purchasers are expected to pay for the goods they have bought within an agreed period of time — 30 days or 60 days, etc. The period of credit would vary from customer to customer and from the company to company and depends on the credit worthiness of the customer, market conditions and competition.

Often customers may not pay within the agreed credit period. This may be due to laxity in credit administration or the inability of the customers to pay.

Consequently, debts are classified as:

- Those over six months; and
- Others.

These are further subdivided into:

- Debts considered good; and
- Debts considered bad and doubtful.

If debts are likely to be bad, they must be provided for or written off. If this is not done, assets will be overstated to the extent of the bad debt. A write off is made only when there is no hope of recovery. Otherwise, a provision is made. Provisions may be specific or they may be general. When amounts are provided on certain identified debts, the provision is termed specific whereas if a provision amounting to a certain percentage of all debts are made, the provision is termed general.

PREPAID EXPENSES

All payments are not made when due. Many payments, such as insurance premiums, rent and service costs are made in advance for a period of time which may be 3 months, 6 months, or even a year. The portion of such expenses that relates to the next accounting period are shown as prepaid expenses in the balance sheet.

CASH AND BANK BALANCES

Cash in hand in petty cash boxes, tills, safes and balances in bank accounts are shown under this heading in the balance sheet.

LOANS AND ADVANCES

These are loans that have been given to other corporations, individuals and employees and are repayable within a certain period of time. This item also includes amounts paid in advance for the supply of goods, materials and services, etc.

OTHER CURRENT ASSETS

Other current assets are all amounts due that are recoverable within the next twelve months. These include claims receivable, interest due on investments, and the like.

Current Liabilities

Current liabilities are amounts due that are payable within the next twelve months. These also include provisions which are amounts set aside for an expense incurred for which the bill has not been received as yet or whose cost has not yet been fully estimated.

TRADE CREDITORS

Trade creditors are those to whom the company owes monies for raw materials and other articles and services used in the manufacture of its products or services. Companies usually purchase these on credit — the credit period depending on the demand for the item, the standing of the company and market practice.

ACCRUED EXPENSES

Certain expenses such as interest on bank overdrafts, telephone costs, electricity and overtime are paid after they have been incurred. This is because they fluctuate and it is not possible to either prepay or accurately anticipate these expenses. However, the expense has been incurred. To recognize this, the expense incurred is estimated based on past trends and known expenses incurred and accrued on the date of the balance sheet.

PROVISIONS

Provisions are amounts set aside from profits for an estimated expense or loss. Certain provisions, such as depreciation and provisions for bad debts, are deducted from the concerned asset itself. For some others, such as claims that may be payable, provisions are made. Other provisions normally seen in balance sheets are those for dividends and taxation.

SUNDRY CREDITORS

Any other amounts due are usually clubbed under the all-embracing title of sundry creditors. These include unclaimed dividends and dues payable to third parties.

Profit and Loss Account

The Profit and Loss Account summarizes the activities of a company during an accounting period which may be a month, a quarter, six months, a year or longer, and the result achieved by the company. It details the income earned by the company, its cost, and the resulting profit or loss. It is, in effect, the performance appraisal not only of the company but also of its management — its competence, foresight and ability to lead.

Sales

This is the amount received or receivable from customers arising from the sales of goods and the provision of services by a company. A sale occurs when the ownership of goods and the consequent risk relating to those goods are passed to the customer in return for consideration, usually cash. In normal circumstances the physical possession of the goods is also transferred at the same time. A sale does not occur when a company places goods at the shop of a dealer with the clear understanding that payment need be made only after the goods are sold failing, which they may be returned. In such a case, the ownership and risks are not transferred to the dealer nor any consideration paid.

Companies do give trade discounts and other incentive discounts to customers to entice them to buy their products. Sales should be accounted for after deducting these discounts. However, cash discount given for early payment is a finance expense and should be shown as an expense and not deducted from sales.

There are many companies which deduct excise duty and other levies from sales. There are others who show this as an expense. It is preferable to deduct these from sales since the sales figures would then reflect the actual markup made by the company on its cost of production.

Other Income

Companies may also receive income from sources other than from the sale of their products or the provision of services. These are usually clubbed together under the heading, other income. The more common items that appear under this title are:

PROFIT FROM THE SALE OF ASSETS

Profit from the sale of investments or assets.

DIVIDENDS

Dividends earned from investments made by the company in the shares of other companies.

RENT

Rent received from commercial buildings and apartments leased from the company.

INTEREST

Interest received on deposits made and loans given to corporate and other bodies.

Expenditure

MATERIALS

Materials are the raw materials and other items used in the manufacture of a company's products. This is also sometimes called the cost of goods sold.

EMPLOYMENT COSTS

The costs of employment are accounted for under this head and would include wages, salaries, bonus, gratuity, contributions made to provident and other funds, welfare expenses, and other employee related expenditure.

Operating and Other Expenses

All other costs incurred in running a company are called operating and other expenses, and include:

1. **Selling expenses:** The cost of advertising, sales commissions, sales promotion expenses and other sales related expenses.
2. **Administration expenses:** Rent of offices and factories, municipal taxes, stationery, telephone and telex costs, electricity charges, insurance, repairs, motor maintenance, and all other expenses incurred to run a company.
3. **Others:** This includes costs that are not strictly administration or selling expenses, such as donations made, losses on the sale of fixed assets or investments, miscellaneous expenditure and the like.

Interest and Finance Charges

A company has to pay interest on monies it borrows. This is normally shown separately as it is a cost distinct from the normal costs incurred in running a business and would vary from company to company. The normal borrowings that a company pays interest on are:

1. Bank overdrafts;
2. Term loans taken for the purchase of machinery or construction of a factory;
3. Fixed deposits from the public;
4. Debentures; and
5. Intercorporate loans.

Depreciation

Depreciation represents the wear and tear incurred by the fixed assets of a company, i.e. the reduction in the value of fixed assets on account of usage. This is also shown separately as the depreciation charge of similar companies in the same industry will differ, depending on the age of the fixed assets and the cost at which they have been bought.

Taxation

Most companies are taxed on the profits that they make. It must be remembered, however, that taxes are payable on the taxable income or profit and this can differ dramatically from the accounting income or profit. This is because many amounts legitimately expensed may not be tax deductible. Conversely, income such as agricultural income is not taxable.

Dividends

Dividends are profits distributed to shareholders. The total profits after tax are not always distributed — a portion is often ploughed back into the company for its future growth and expansion. Dividends paid during the year in anticipation of profits are known as interim dividends. The final dividend is usually declared after the results for the period have been determined. The final dividend is proposed at the annual general meeting of the company and paid after the approval of the shareholders.

Transfer to Reserves

The transfer to reserves is the profit ploughed back into the company. This may be done to finance working capital, expansion, fixed assets or for some other purpose. These are revenue reserves and can be distributed to shareholders as dividends.

Contingent Liabilities

Contingent liabilities are liabilities that may arise upon the happening of an event. It is uncertain, however, whether the event itself may occur. This is why these are not provided for and shown as an actual liability in the balance sheet. Contingent liabilities are detailed in the financial statements as a note to inform the readers of possible future liabilities while arriving at an opinion about the company. The contingent liabilities one normally encounters are:

- Bills discounted with banks — these may crystallize into active liabilities if the bills are dishonoured.

- Gratuity to employees not provided for.
- Legal suits against the company not provided for.
- Claims against a company not acknowledged or accepted.
- Excise claims against the company.

Schedules and Notes to the Accounts

The schedules and notes to the accounts are an integral part of the financial statements of a company and it is important that they be read along with the financial statements. Most people avoid reading these. They do so at their own risk as these provide vital clues and information.

Schedules

The schedules detail pertinent information about the items of balance sheet and profit & loss account. It also details information about sales, manufacturing costs, administration costs, interest, and other income and expenses. This information is vital for the analysis of financial statements. The schedules enable an investor to determine which expenses increased and seek the reasons for this. Similarly, investors would be able to find out the reasons for the increase or decrease in sales and the products that are sales leaders. The schedules even give details of stocks and sales, particulars of capacity and productions, and much other useful information.

Notes

The notes to the accounts are even more important than the schedules because it is here that very important information relating to the company is stated. Notes can effectively be divided into:

1. Accounting Policies,
2. Contingent Liabilities, and
3. Others.

Accounting Policies

All companies follow certain accounting principles and these may differ from those of other entities. As a consequence, the profit earned might differ. Companies have also been known to change (normally increase) their profit by changing the accounting policies. For instance, in one of Tata Iron and Steel Company's annual reports it was stated among other things, "There has been a change in the method of accounting relating to interest on borrowings used for capital expenditure. While such interest was fully written off in the previous years, interest charges incurred during the year have been capitalized for the period upto the date from which the assets have been put to use. Accordingly, expenditure transferred to capital account includes an amount of ₹ 46.63 crore towards interest capitalized. The profit before taxes for the year after the consequential adjustments of depreciation of ₹ 0.12 crore is therefore higher by ₹ 46.51 crore than what it would have been had the previous basis been followed." This means that by changing an accounting policy. TISCO was able to increase its income by ₹ 46 crore. There could be similar notes on other items in the financial statements.

The accounting policies normally detailed in the notes relate to:

1. How sales are accounted.
2. What the research and development costs are.
3. How the gratuity liability is expensed.
4. How fixed assets are valued.
5. How depreciation is calculated.
6. How stock, including finished goods, work in progress, raw materials and consumable goods are valued.
7. How investments are stated in the balance sheet.
8. How foreign exchange has been translated.

Contingent Liabilities

As noted earlier, contingent liabilities relate to liabilities that might crystallize upon the happening of an uncertain event. All contingent liabilities are detailed in the notes to the accounts and it would be wise to read these as they give valuable insights. The more common contingent liabilities that one comes across in the financial statements of companies are:

1. Outstanding guarantees.

2. Outstanding letters of credit.
3. Outstanding bills discounted.
4. Claims against the company not acknowledged as debts.
5. Claim for taxes.
6. Cheques discounted.
7. Uncalled liability on partly paid shares and debentures.

Others

It must be appreciated that the purpose of notes to the accounts is to inform the reader more fully. Consequently, they detail all pertinent factors which affect, or will affect, the company and its results. Often as a consequence, adjustments may need to be made to the accounts to unearth the true results.

As a hypothetical example, Note 6 of Puniya Ltd.'s Annual Report for 2014-2015 stated: "The Company has during the year credited an amount of ₹ 132.14 lakh to surplus on sale of assets (Schedule No. 13) which included an amount of ₹ 112.88 lakh being the excess of sale price over the original cost of the fixed assets. Till the accounting year 2013-2014, such excess over the original cost was credited to capital reserve. Had the Company followed the earlier method of accounting the profit for the year would have been lower by ₹ 112.88 lakh." This suggests that the company had changed its accounting policy in order to increase its profits. The profit before tax that year (year ended 31 March 2015) was ₹ 108.12 lakh (previous year ₹ 309.80 lakh). Had this adjustment not been made, the company would have suffered a loss of ₹ 4.76 lakh. The company had also withdrawn ₹ 35.34 lakh from the revaluation reserve. It was also stated in that company's annual report that "no provision had been made for ₹ 16.39 lakh being the fall in the breakup value of unquoted shares in wholly owned subsidiary companies" and "the income tax liability amounting to ₹ 36.41 lakh relating to prior years has been adjusted against the profits transferred to the General Reserve in the respective years." The latter points out that the tax change had been adjusted directly with reserves as opposed to routing it through the Profit and Loss account. Had that been done the profit after tax would have further reduced. Similar comments are made in the notes to the accounts of other companies also.

The more common notes one comes across are:

- Whether provisions for known or likely losses have been made.
- Estimated value of contracts outstanding.
- Interest not provided for.
- Arrangements agreed by the company with third parties.
- Agreement with labour.

The importance of these notes cannot be overstressed. It is imperative that investors read these carefully.

~

Chapter 34

~

Ratio Analysis for Investment

It is in the analysis of financial statements that ratios come into their own. They help investors to:

- Analyze the performance of a company and compare it with that of other similar companies.
- Determine the relative weaknesses and strengths of a company — whether it is profitable and financially sound, and whether its condition is improving or deteriorating.
- Fulfil the needs of those in knowing a company's financial position.

Ratios really put figures into perspective. It is difficult to see how a company is doing by looking at a large number of figures. Ratios summarize the figures in a form that is easily understood, interpreted and used.

Ratios express a relationship between one figure and another. It is important that the relationship between the figures is real. Otherwise, the result would be meaningless and serve no purpose. For example, a ratio expressing the cost of sales as a percentage of investments is of no consequence as there is no commonality between the figures whereas a ratio that expresses gross profit as a percentage of sales indicates the markup made on the cost of purchases or the margin earned by the company.

To interpret ratios properly, we must ensure that the ratios being measured are consistent and valid. At a time of rising prices, a current ratio wherein inventories are valued under the "last in first out" method is meaningless. Similarly, in comparing results, if the length of the periods being compared is different or if there is a large non-recurring income or expense, the ratios calculated would be misleading. If ratios are used to evaluate operating performance extraordinary items should be excluded as they are non-recurring and do not reflect normal performance. In truth, the usefulness of ratios is entirely dependent on their intelligent and skillful interpretation.

It is also important when interpreting ratios, to be aware of the factors that affect the company, such as its management policy, the industry, general business conditions and the state of the economy. Otherwise, the conclusions arrived at can be incorrect

Ratios are strong pointers. They do not necessarily give answers. They reveal situations and raise questions. Answers lie behind the ratios. Ratios should be looked at as a starting point and whether a ratio is good or bad depends on the company, the industry, the economy and can be, if logically and intelligently interpreted, a valuable tool for the investing public.

Although there are many ratios that are used by analysts to microscopically examine the performance and future potential of companies, I intend to highlight those ratios which are of importance to investors.

Market Value Ratios

The market value indicators are important to investors. They indicate the reputation of a company in financial circles and the length of time it will take for their investment to be recouped. It gives the company's management an idea of what investors and financial experts think of the company's past performance and future prospects. If a firm's liquidity, asset management, debt management and profitability ratios are high then its market value ratios and stock price will also be high.

Price / Earnings

The price / earnings (P/E) ratio shows how long it would take to recover the cost of an investment (*see* Illustration 34.1). It is calculated as follows:

$$\text{Price / Earnings ratio} = \frac{\text{Market price per share}}{\text{Dividend per share}}$$

Illustration 34.1

The dividend paid for the year ended 31 March 20xx by Homedale Tea Estates Limited was ₹ 10. The market value of a ₹ 10 share of the company was ₹ 280. The price / earning ratio is:

280 / 10 = 28

This means that it would take an investor 28 years to get back his investment.

Usually the price/earnings ratio of long, well established and financially sound companies are high, whereas in weaker ones, as the returns commensurate with the risks are higher, the price/earnings ratio is low. It is interesting to note that while abroad the P/E ratio of companies are between 13 to 16, the P/E of Indian companies (even the well established ones) are usually over 20. The reason supporting this is that India is developing rapidly and as profits begin to become larger price earnings ratios will fall.

Market to Book

The market to book ratio indicates the value investors place on the company. It can also suggest in certain situations that the assets of a company are understated (*see* Illustration 34.2). The market to book ratio is calculated as follows:

$$\text{Market to book ratio} = \frac{\text{Market price per share}}{\text{Book value per share}}$$

Illustration 34.2

On 28 June 20xx, the market price per share of Nivya Ltd. was ₹ 80. The book value of its share was ₹ 30. Its market/book value was:

80 / 30 = 2.67

The company's value in the market place is 167 per cent higher than its book value. This may be because:

- Its assets are understated.
- Its prospects are good and investors believe that its earnings and value would grow.

Market value ratios can be misleading because in a boom period, the ratios may be high, while in a depression they may be low. Their importance to investors is thus of limited value as they do not reveal the profitability or efficiency of a company but merely indicates the company's reputation in the market place.

It should also be stressed that the book values are based on historical costs and balance sheets are not intended to be statements of current value. Therefore, any conclusion drawn from comparisons of book value to market value should be treated with some caution.

Earnings Ratio

The earnings per share ratio, indicates the earnings available per ordinary share. It is an indicator which enables investors and shareholders to judge the earnings per share of a company and is often considered an indicator of profitability.

Earnings per Share (EPS)

The earnings per share shows an investor the earnings attributable to an ordinary share in a year (*see* Illustration 34.3).

$$\text{Earnings per share} = \frac{\text{Income attributable to ordinary shareholders}}{\text{Weighted average of ordinary share}}$$

Illustration 34.3

In 200x, the income attributable to the shareholders of Nikhila Ltd. was ₹ 50,00,000. On 1 January 200x, the company had a balance of 250,000 ordinary shares of ₹ 10 each.

$$\text{E.P.S.} = \frac{50,00\,000}{2,50,000} = ₹\ 20 \text{ per share}$$

If on 30 June 200x, the company had issued a further 250,000 shares and the earnings per share for 200x would be:

$$\text{Diluted E.P.S.} = \frac{50,00,000}{2,50,000 + \frac{6 \text{ months} \times 2,50,000}{12 \text{ months}}} = ₹\ 13.33 \text{ per share}$$

Contd...

Illustration 34.3 *(. . . contd)*

This ratio has been further varied to show the fully diluted earnings per share. This is the earnings per share that would occur if all the share options, warrants and convertible securities outstanding at the end of the accounting period were exchanged for ordinary shares.

The earnings per share ratio has been criticized as a measure of profitability on the argument that it does not consider the amount of assets, finance or capital required to generate a particular amount of income.

Dividend Payout

The dividend payout ratio shows the amount of dividend paid out of earnings. It gives an indication of the amount of profit put back into the company and is an important ratio when assessing the long term prospects of a company (*see* Illustration 34.4):

$$\text{Dividend payout ratio} = \frac{\text{Dividend}}{\text{Net Income}}$$

Illustration 34.4

In 200x, the net income of Divya Ltd. was ₹ 5,80,000 and the dividend paid by the company was ₹ 2,60,000. The dividend payout ratio is:

$$\frac{2{,}60{,}000}{5{,}80{,}000} = 0.448$$

This shows that the company is paying out nearly 45% of its income as dividend. This is a fairly high payout and can be worrying, as in difficult years the company could have problems of liquidity. Furthermore, there may not be adequate funds for expansion when the need arises.

The earnings ratios are not indicators of the profitability of a company, such as the amount of income ploughed back into the company and the earnings per share earned. It indicates the direction the company intends to go — whether it believes in expansion from internally generated funds or from borrowed funds. This, in turn, will determine the relative safety of funds lent to it.

Leverage or Gearing Ratios

Leverage or gearing or coverage as it is sometimes called is a term used to describe the extent assets are covered by liabilities. Highly leveraged companies can afford less reduction in asset values at the time of liquidation. This is also a measure of the extent to which loans and liabilities are a source of funds. Creditors look to equity or owners' funds to determine the owners' stake in the company, and the owners' abiding commitment in order to provide them with a margin of safety. If the owners have provided only a small proportion of the finance of the company, the major risks are borne by the creditors. The owners, by financing the company with outside loans, control the firm with limited investments.

Leverage indicates the level of financial risk which is borne in addition to the business risk. If a company is very dependent on borrowed funds, profits will be high during a good year. In a bad year they will be low and could even be at a loss. This is illustrated in Table 34.1.

It will be observed from Table 34.1 that so long as the return or the rate of profits exceed the cost of borrowed funds, the highly leveraged company is more profitable. However, should the trend reverse, should sales decrease or costs increase or depression sets in, the income generated by highly leveraged firms are used almost entirely to service their debt and the return to the shareholders become negligible.

In short, if a company earns more on borrowed funds than it pays in interest, the return on owner's funds are magnified. If the operating income is low, the leverage will reduce the equity return below the rate of return on assets. In this instance return on equity is measured as:

$$\text{Return on equity} = \frac{\text{Income available ordinary shareholders}}{\text{Ordinary shares}}$$

Table: 34.1

Returns for Different Levels of Leverage

(Rupees Crores)

	Company A	Company B	Company C
Share Capital	20	80	100
Borrowed funds at 15% p.a.	80	20	--
	100	100	100
GOOD YEAR			
Earning before interest & tax	50	50	50
Interest at 15% p.a.	12	3	--
	38	47	50
Tax at 50%	19	23.5	25
	19	23.5	25
Return after tax (%)	95	29.4	25
REASONABLE YEAR			
Earning before interest & tax	30	30	30
Interest at 15% p.a.	12	3	--
	18	27	30
Tax at 50%	9	13.5	15
	9	13.5	15
Return after tax (%)	45	16.9	15
BAD YEAR			
Earning before interest & tax	12	12	12
Interest at 15% p.a.	12	3	--
		9	12
Tax at 50%	--	4.5	6
	--	4.5	6
Return after tax (%)		5.6	6

As is obvious from Table 34.1, companies with low amount of debt have less risk of a loss when the economy is in recession and demand is low. Similarly, they have also lower expected returns when the economy booms. Highly leveraged companies run the risk of large losses, but they have the opportunity of earning high profits.

Liabilities to Assets Ratio

This ratio, a relatively pure measure of asset coverage, indicates the total funds provided by creditors to the business; the extent the firm is financed by persons or entities other than shareholders. Liabilities in this connection include both current and long-term liabilities. Assets on the other hand are total assets, less intangibles such as goodwill and deferred assets (*see* Illustration 34.5).

$$\text{Liabilities to assets ratio} = \frac{\text{total liabilities}}{\text{total assets}}$$

Illustration 34.5

Total liabilities	150
Shareholders' equity	50
	200
Current assets	130
Fixed Assets	60
Intangible assets	10
	200

Liabilities to assets ratio = 150/190 = 0.789

Assets could be sold at 78.9% of their book value and the company can still meet its commitments.

Debt to Networth Ratio

The debt to networth ratio indicates the extent a company is financed by outside or borrowed funds. Debt would include subordinated debt as well as senior debt and capital leases. Networth is arrived at by deducting intangible assets from the shareholder's equity.

$$\text{Debt to networth ratio} = \frac{\text{Debt}}{\text{Net worth}}$$

A ratio of 3 would indicate that for every ₹ 3 borrowed, the shareholders have only ₹ 1/- interest in the company. In a highly leveraged company, profits may be inadequate during a bad year. Additionally, they can face difficulty in obtaining refinance.

Other Ratios

Other leverage ratios are:

1. The liabilities to net worth ratio which measures the extent a company is financed by liabilities.
2. Incremental leverage which measure the additional gearing required to finance the growth of the company.

The leverage ratios indicate whether a company has over-borrowed, whether it has the capacity to obtain additional funds and the effects on its leverage profits. Leverage must be examined and studied in detail prior to investing in a company.

The importance of leverage is appreciated if a company borrows extensively, during a period of growth; it can collapse should a recession occur and sales and profits fall. Furthermore, a higher leveraged company has less capacity to obtain refinance.

Debt Service Capacity Ratios

Investors must be concerned whether a company can service its debts, i.e. generate enough profits to be able to pay the interest on its loans.

The basic assumption in the debt capacity ratios is that a company is a going concern and that the debt will be repaid out of internally generated funds and not from the sale of assets or additional borrowings. The ratios, therefore, indicate the relationships between cash flow (internally generated funds) and the company's liabilities.

Debt Coverage

The debt coverage ratio indicates the time it would take for a company to repay its short and long term debt from internally generated funds or profits.

In this context, internally generated funds are the net profit after tax, non-cash expenses such as depreciation less non-cash income such as the profit from the sale of fixed assets. Debts would include bank overdrafts, notes payable (both short and long term) and term loans. In many instances this ratio is calculated, including long-term debentures as debt. Internally generated funds are divided by debt or borrowed funds.

$$\text{Debt coverage ratio} = \frac{\text{Internally generated funds}}{\text{Average debt}}$$

A ratio of 0.108, for example, indicates that it would take a company 9.25 years to repay its borrowed funds (debts) from its internally generated funds.

Liability Coverage

The liability coverage ratio is used to determine the time a company would take to pay off all its liabilities from internally generated funds. This assumes that liabilities will not be liquidated from additional borrowings or from the sale of assets. It is calculated by dividing internally generated funds by average total liabilities.

$$\text{Liability coverage ratio} = \frac{\text{Internally generated funds}}{\text{Total average liabilities}}$$

A ratio is 0.20, for example, it would indicate that the company would pay off all its liabilities in 5 years. On the other hand, a ratio of 0.125 would mean that it would take the company 8 years to pay off its liabilities in full.

This ratio is often calculated by considering only the liabilities at the date of the balance sheet on the argument that the thing to be considered is the time that it would take to pay off the total liabilities at a particular time.

The liability coverage ratio is susceptible to window dressing, as liabilities on the balance sheet date can be reduced either by paying them or by suppressing them.

Interest Cover

Interest cover, a ratio of prime importance, measures whether a company has adequate profits to meet the interest payments on its obligations. It is arrived at by dividing the company's earnings before interest and tax (EBIT) by its interest expense.

$$\text{Interest cover ratio} = \frac{\text{Earnings before interest \& tax}}{\text{Average expense}}$$

A cover ratio of 2, for example, would indicate that the company's earnings before interest expense are twice that of its interest expense and it can, therefore, meet its obligations. This ratio is very important as it reveals whether the profits of a company are sufficient to meet its interest commitments.

Debt service ratios are important to determine whether a company has the capacity or ability to service its debts and repay its liabilities.

Profitability Ratios

Profitability ratios indicate a company's profitability in relation to that of other companies within the industry; to previous years; to other companies in other industries, and provide a measure of the management's effectiveness as shown by the returns generated through sales and investments.

These ratios must be considered in relation to rates of inflation and the cost of capital and borrowings.

Trends in ratios should be evaluated as possible indications of future development.

As large variations in asset and liability figures can distort the ratios quite materially, the ratios should be calculated on average assets or liabilities. The logic of this is evident when one considers the income earned is an average figure earned over the whole year and not an amount earned on a particular date.

Return on Total Assets

The return on total assets (ROTA) allows one to determine whether:

- The margin earned on sales is reasonable.
- The assets of the company are adequately and effectively used.
- The interest payments made by the company are too high.

This, as a measure, should be used to compare performance between companies within an industry and with previous years. This is computed in the following manner:

$$\text{ROTA} = \frac{\text{Net income after tax}}{\text{Average total assets}}$$

The investor must determine whether the return is adequate.

Return on Common Equity (Shares)

The return on common equity (ROCE) measures the ratio of return to shareholders on their investment. It enables one to check whether the return on an investment is better than other alternatives available. This is calculated by expressing (as a percentage of shareholders' funds), net profit after tax less dividend on preference stock and minority interest.

$$\text{ROCE} = \text{Net income after tax} - \text{minority interest} - \frac{\text{dividend on preference stock}}{\text{average shareholders' equity}}$$

If alternative investments are available that yield a return in excess of this and carry a higher risk, it would indicate that the company's profitability is low.

As the major aim of a commercial enterprise is profit, the profitability ratios are among the more important group of ratios and must always be examined in depth. All changes in these ratios must be looked into, as these could be indicators of the company's long term results.

It should be remembered, however, that in comparing profitability, a company with higher profitability ratios is not necessarily better. In order to increase sales and profits in actual money terms, companies often trade or sell their goods at lower prices.

Liquidity Ratios

One of the first things an investor needs to know about a company is whether it can pay its currently maturing financial obligations and also if it has enough cash to meet its operational requirements. If not, it may be forced to sell its more important assets at a loss, and, in extreme cases, go into liquidation.

Current Ratio

The most common measure of liquidity is the current ratio. This is computed by dividing current assets by current liabilities.

$$\text{Current ratio} = \frac{\text{Current assets}}{\text{Current liabilities}}$$

Ideally the ratio should be around 2:1.

Quick or Acid Test

The quick or acid test is applied to examine whether a company has adequate cash or cash equivalents to meet its current obligations without having to resort to liquidating non-cash assets, such as stocks. This ratio aims to emphasize that the immediate sale of non-cash items such as stocks could be at less than its stated value, i.e. at a loss (distress sale). It, therefore, checks whether the company has adequate cash or easily realizable assets.

The quick ratio is calculated by dividing cash, marketable securities and debtors by current liabilities.

$$\text{Quick ratio} = \frac{\text{Cash and cash equivalent}}{\text{Current liabilities}}$$

The ratio should ideally be 1:1 or a little higher

As a company begins to experience financial difficulties, it pays its bills more slowly. This results in the build-up of current liabilities. If current liabilities are rising faster than the build up of current assets, it could result in the company facing financial trouble and its inability to meet its obligations. Hence, a deterioration in the current ratio should cause concern.

However, a negative ratio need not necessarily be bad. Many concerns which have very high stock turnover and sell for cash, normally have high current liabilities compared with current assets. This does not mean that these are concerns.

Asset Management and Efficiency Ratios

Asset management of efficiency ratios are calculated to determine how effectively a company is managing its assets. It allows one to consider and examine whether the total amount of each type of asset a company has is reasonable, too high or too low in the light of current and forecasted operating needs. In order to purchase assets, companies may need to obtain additional external finance. Thus, if there are more assets than necessary, the interest expense would be high and profits lower than otherwise. Conversely, should there be fewer assets than required, the company's operations would not be as efficient as possible.

Asset management ratios assume that sales volumes are related to assets over time. Ratios can be used to assess trends and the efficiency with which the management of a company utilizes its assets. This can be compared with that of the rest of the industry, and with other companies. It should be remembered that a high asset turnover is not necessarily indicative of a high return on investments. It could indicate that a company is not keeping adequate levels of assets, something which could adversely affect its performance in the long run.

Stock Turnover

The stock turnover ratio measures the number of times the inventory is turned over in a year, and the quantum of stock held to support sales. This ratio is calculated by either.

$$\text{Stock turnover ratio} = \frac{\text{Cost of goods sold}}{\text{Average stock}}$$

$$= \text{Times stock turned over}$$

$$\text{Stock turnover ratio} = \frac{365 \text{ days} \times \text{Average stock}}{\text{Cost of goods sold}}$$

$$= \text{Stock measured in days of sale.}$$

A ratio of 6 times or 60 days indicates that there is enough stock to support sales for 60 days.

This ratio enables one to determine whether the company holds excessive stocks. Excessive stocks are unproductive and represent an investment with a low or zero rate of return. Conversely, if a company has less stock then it should, it could result in a loss of customers which would offset the advantage of having low stock.

Average Collection Period

The average collection period represents the length of time a company must wait after making a sale before it actually receives cash from its customers. The ratio is calculated as follow:

$$\text{Average collection period ratio} = \frac{\text{Average sales}}{\text{Average sales per day}}$$

or

$$\text{Average collection period ratio} = \frac{\text{Average debts}}{\text{Sales}} \times 365$$

This ratio is important in assessing the effectiveness of credit administration and the demand for the company's product. An increasing ratio could suggest that the company is experiencing difficulties in collecting debts.

This could be an early warning sign for large bad debts.

Asset management ratios reflect the efficiency of a management and its ability to manage the assets of a company. It indicates the effectiveness of a company's credit policies, the demand for its products and can reflect to an extent whether it is having difficulty in meeting its obligations. The asset management ratios are, therefore, important in understanding a company.

Limitations of Ratio Analysis

Ratio analysis provides an indication of a company's profitability, liquidity, leverage and solvency. But ratios do not provide answers; they are merely a guide to the areas of a company's weaknesses and strengths.

However, ratio analysis is difficult and there are many limitations:

- Many firms are very diversified and engaged in a number of different activities. This makes it difficult to develop a meaningful set of averages in order to compare performance.
- A ratio can be purposely distorted by a company to make it look better than it actually is. For example, a company could sell its debts at a discount for cash and as a result its collection ratio of debtors would be low, leading one to believe its efficiency to be greater than it actually is.
- In order to state whether a ratio is good or bad it must be interpreted intelligently. A high current ratio may indicate, on the one hand, a liquidity position (which is positive) or excessive liquid cash (which is negative).
- It is difficult to use ratios to compare companies because they very often follow different accounting principles. One company may

value stock under "the last in first out" principle, while another may follow the "first in first out" principle. Similarly, one company may depreciate assets under the straight-line method, while its competitor may use accelerated depreciation.

It is important to remember that prior to the ratios being computed, one must examine the financial statements and their accompanying notes and ensure that, in comparing performance and strengths, adjustments are made for variations from one year to the next. Some questions that should be asked and things that must be looked for are:

- Do sales actually reflect economic reality?
- Has any change in accounting principles taken place? And if so, what is its effect on the company's results and assets?
- Have any debts been sold with recourse?
- Does the company own a finance company that is un-consolidated and what would be the effect on the company if it were consolidated?
- Are pension and gratuity funds totally funded?
- Are there any contingent liabilities that must be accounted for?
- Is there any non-recurring income or expense?

It is also important to remember that a company may have some bad ratios and some good. It is incorrect to pass judgment on a company by looking at only one set of ratios. The ratios need to be seen altogether to obtain a true picture of how a company is performing.

~

Conclusion

This revision has been an exhilarating experience because in the last one-and-a-half-decade the face of Indian investing has changed. This revision thus gave me an opportunity to re-look at the conclusions I had arrived at then and the points I wished to make. I find that they are still valid. Nothing has really changed.

A point I do wish to emphasize is that the market, while it is exciting, must be approached with some caution. One must invest based on one's risk appetite and after having studied the market. The money one invests in the market should be the excess one has and not one's entire savings. One must also be prepared to be patient. Investing in shares should be for the long term. One must also remember that history repeats itself and what goes up does come down too.

Investing should be done in stages. Not in one fell swoop. I echo Hesiod's comment, "If you should put even a little, and do this often enough, soon this too would become big."

And with regard to the excitement and fun of the market I'd like to quote Walter Knowleton Gutman, "There is nothing like a ticker tape except a woman; nothing that promises hour after hour, day after day such sudden development; nothing that disappoints so often or occasionally with such unbelievable, passionate magnificence."

I do hope you have enjoyed this book and will profit from it.

~

Quiz 1

~

What Kind of an Investor are You?

There are many kinds of investors. Speculators are intent on making money fast; balanced mature investors wish to see the value of their investments rise steadily, while sober, prudent investors are reluctant to take any risks.

The following quiz is designed to find out the kind of person you are whether a gambler, or a risk averse person.

1. You have ₹ 1,00,000 in hand, which of the following would you do with it?

(a) Purchase equity shares of companies.
(b) Purchase government bonds.
(c) Place it in fixed deposits with companies.

2. If you need to have ₹ 5,00,000 in six months time for a long dreamed of holiday how are you likely to make it?

(a) By buying and selling shares.
(b) By working harder and longer hours and by saving.
(c) By selling an item/items of value.

3. Which of the following situations is likely to give you the most satisfaction?

(a) You win ₹ 5,00,000 in a lottery.
(b) You win ₹ 5,00,000 as a prize from a competition or contest that you had entered.

(c) You gain ₹ 5,00,000 from an old uncle.
(d) It does not matter. Any of the above would do. You are not concerned with how you get the ₹ 5,00,000. You are happy that you have got it.

4. A few weeks after your purchase of some shares, they fall in value by 20% as part of a general trend due to various rumours. Would you:
(a) Sell the shares you have in the expectation of the market value falling further?
(b) Hold on to them in the belief that they will rise?
(c) Buy more as you feel the share is under-priced and you are sure to make a killing when the price rises again?

5. It is rumoured that the forthcoming budget would bear good news for industry and that share prices will boom. Would you:
(a) In anticipation begin buying as many shares as you can with whatever money you have in hand?
(b) Buy as many shares as you can and then borrow more money from others to buy some more?
(c) Wait and see what happens before you commit your funds?

6. The budget has been announced and it offers no encouragement to industry. As a consequence there is a small fall in the prices. Would you:
(a) Wait and hold on to your investment as you are sure prices will rise again to earlier levels?
(b) Sell the shares you hold and cut your losses?
(c) Buy more shares as you believe the company you have invested in is sound and that the price will rise?

7. A friend of yours comes to you with a "hot tip" that the price of the shares of a certain not very well known company is likely to increase by at least 50% in 3 months time. Would you:
(a) Buy as much as you can, using all the money you have at your disposal?
(b) Buy as many as you can and borrow some money and purchase more?
(c) Do nothing?

8. The shares that you purchased a few months ago have increased in value by 50%. Assuming you have no other details on the performance and future of the company, would you:
(a) Sell a portion of it and hold on to the balance?
(b) Sell all the shares?
(c) Do nothing. Hold on to the shares as you feel the shares will further increase in prices?
(d) Buy more as the prices would go higher?

9. A company that you have invested in is in a state of turmoil. The industry is going through a difficult time. Management has changed. However, the prices have been reasonably stable. Would you:
(a) Sell as you are worried about the change of management and the industry situation?
(b) Keep still as you believe in the company?
(c) Buy more as you feel the share is under-priced?

10. Which would give you greater pleasure?
(a) Doubling your money in six months by purchasing and selling shares.
(b) Finding that as you had placed all your money in low interest bearing government securities and deposits in scheduled banks, your money stayed intact whereas others who had purchased shares had found the value of their share fell by 50%.

11. Which would you prefer to do:
(a) Invest in mutual funds that are managed by professional portfolio managers?
(b) Invest in the shares of companies as you feel their price would rise much faster?

12. Your work for an electronics company that was started four years earlier by a group of NRI Investors. The company's products have been well accepted. Demand is good and increasing and the company is now thinking of setting up another factory. To finance this expansion, the company proposes to issue shares to the public.

As an employee you are eligible for a preferential firm allotment of up to 500 shares. How many shares would you buy:

(a) All 500 shares offered?
(b) Only 300 shares out of the 500 shares offered?
(c) None at all?

13. A friend of yours, is about to start a business venture and has offered you an opportunity to invest in the company he is about to promote. The company intends to warehouse, outside the city limits, electrical goods for sale at competitive prices. The idea is new and if successful the company is likely to make large profits. If not the company would make large losses. The chance of success is about 25 per cent. Would you invest:

(a) As much money as you can?
(b) Nothing at all?
(c) Half the money that you have available?

14. You go to the races with ₹ 1,00,000. In the first four races you lose ₹ 50,000. What will you do?

(a) Nothing — you will cut your losses and call its quits.
(b) You will bet another ₹ 3,000 and if you lose that, you'll stop.
(c) You'll carry on betting till you have either recouped your losses or lost the remaining ₹ 50,000.

15. You inherit a flat in a fashionable suburb of Mumbai. As you have another flat you don't actually need it. The flat can be rented out to excellent companies but once rented out the chances of getting it back are remote. The value of the flat is likely to increase faster than the rate of inflation. Would you:

(a) Keep the flat empty?
(b) Sell the flat and invest the money in income yielding shares?
(c) Rent the flat out for a rent and take a deposit on it?

16. It is predicted that there is likely to be a huge stock market crash in the next year. Would you:

(a) Sell all the shares that you have and purchase hard assets such as gold/real estate, etc.?
(b) Sell half the shares that you have and invest them in hard assets and in fixed deposits with banks?

(c) Hold on to your shares. No crash is likely to take place. This is just a panic being created?

17. A building is coming up in your locality which you know will be much sought after and in demand. You are offered a flat in the building which you know you will be above to sell at a 40% profit in 6 months Would you:

(a) Purchase the flat and sell it in six months?
(b) Not buy it as you are not in the real estate business?

18. Which would you rather do?

(a) Invest all your money in fixed deposits, government backed debentures and units of the Unit Trust of India.
(b) Invest all your money in the shares of companies.
(c) Invest all your money in mixture of fixed deposits in banks and the shares of strong multinational blue chip companies.

19. You live in a house that your father originally took on rent for a very nominal sum fifty years ago. The landlord wishes to construct flats and has approached you with various options, which would you choose

(a) Two flats would be given to you free of cost in the new building when constructed.
(b) ₹ 100 lakh in cash which is the market value of the tenancy rights.
(c) Neither, you wish to carry on living there.

20. You are playing a game of porker with friends and you have won ₹ 1,00,000. You have now the following options which would you choose:

(a) Stop playing.
(b) Carry on playing regardless. You are on a lucky streak and nothing can stop you now.
(c) Play on till you lose the ₹ 1,000 that you're won. Then call it a day.

Answers of Quiz 1

Let us now find out the kind of investor you are whether you are reckless, a speculator or just plain cautious. Add up the points listed for each answer that you made:

	Your Answer (a/b/c/d)	Your Score
1. (a) 4, (b) 1, (c) 2	☐	☐
2. (a) 6, (b) 1, (c) 3	☐	☐
3. (a) 3, (b) 2, (c) 5, (d) 1	☐	☐
4. (a) 1, (b) 3, (c) 5	☐	☐
5. (a) 3, (b) 5, (c) 1	☐	☐
6. (a) 3, (b) 1, (c) 5	☐	☐
7. (a) 4, (b) 5, (c) 1	☐	☐
8. (a) 2, (b) 1, (c) 3, (d) 5	☐	☐
9. (a) 1, (b) 3, (c) 5	☐	☐
10. (a) 3, (b) 2	☐	☐
11. (a) 2, (b) 4	☐	☐
12. (a) 5, (b) 3, (c) 1	☐	☐
13. (a) 5, (b) 1, (c) 3	☐	☐
14. (a) 1, (b) 3, (c) 5	☐	☐
15. (a) 1, (b) 3, (c) 2	☐	☐
16. (a) 1, (b) 2, (c) 3	☐	☐
17. (a) 3, (b) 1	☐	☐
18. (a) 1, (b) 5, (c) 3	☐	☐
19. (a) 2, (b) 3, (c) 1	☐	☐
20. (a) 1, (b) 3, (c) 5	☐	☐
Your total		

If you scored below 41:

You are averse to risk taking. You prefer to place your money in safe investments and sleep soundly at night. Speculation and excitement is not your cup of tea.

If you scored between 41 and 60:

You are an investor who believes in evaluating alternatives before investing. You will not hastily do anything and will follow your head and not your heart. You are often accused of being cold and calculating. That you are not. It is just that you wish to know before your plunge.

If you scored more than 60:

You are the eternal optimist. You believe in taking risks and in the rewards that may accrue. You seek the glamour, the glory and the spoils and are prepared to lose everything in this quest.

~

Quiz 2

~

Have You Got the Right Shares

This is a quiz for individuals who either purchase shares of companies or are seriously considering purchasing equity shares. It is designed to assist you in deciding the shares that you should buy taking into consideration your interests, your habits and your access to information.

Read on the check whether, your portfolio is compatible with you.

Question 1

You have received a bonus of ₹ 10,00,000 for your excellent performance. What would you do with this money?

(a) Place it in a fixed deposit for five years in a bank.
(b) Purchase shares in a large multinational company.
(c) Purchase debentures issued by a public sector company.
(d) Purchase various household appliances that you have been wanting for some time.
(e) Take the family for a holiday abroad.

Question 2

If you could spend an afternoon with any one of the following individuals, whom would you prefer to spend it with?

(a) A politician.
(b) A businessman.

(c) An actor.
(d) An investment consultant.

Question 3

You are at the airport and you decide to purchase a book to read on flight. Which of the following would you buy?
(a) A romantic novel.
(b) A detective story.
(c) A novel.
(d) A murder thriller.
(e) A book on management.
(f) A book on investments.

Question 4

When you meet friends at parties or on other occasions do you discuss share prices, the recent performance of companies or the like?
(a) No, never.
(b) Sometime.
(c) Fairly frequently.
(d) Always.

Question 5

Do you have a portfolio of:
(a) Under 10 shares?
(b) 10 to 20 shares?
(c) Over 25 shares?

Question 6

Is your investment in shares:
(a) ₹ 20,000 and below?
(b) ₹ 20,000 to ₹ 50,000?
(c) ₹ 50,000 to ₹ 2,00,000?
(d) Over ₹ 2,00,000?

Question 7

In regard to your investments in shares are they:
(a) Nearly all concentrated in one or two companies?
(b) Spread evenly between a number of companies?

(c) In no specific pattern?

Question 8

Do you subscribe to any financial newspaper?

(a) None.
(b) One.
(c) More than one.

Question 9

How many business or finance magazines do you read regularly?

(a) One a month.
(b) Two a month.
(c) More than two a month.
(d) None.

Question 10

Every morning at the time of reading your newspaper when you reach financial pages and stock market information:

(a) Do you ignore them and go onto the sports section?
(b) Look at the movement in the shares you have invested in and ignore the rest?
(c) Spend some time analyzing the trends, studying the movement in prices and reading the information given on companies?

Question 11

Do you have access to information relating to the performance of companies prior to their becoming general knowledge?

(a) No, never.
(b) Very seldom.
(c) Often.

Question 12

When you receive the annual reports of companies do you:

(a) Glance through the picture, look at the dividend and then put it aside?
(b) Not even open it?
(c) Read it in detail?

Question 13

Have you acquired the shares that you have:

(a) From a friend?
(b) By inheritance?
(c) Through public issues?
(d) Through a broker?

Question 14

You wish to purchase 1,000 shares of Nivya Limited. Do you buy them through:

(a) A regular broker who handles all your purchases?
(b) A broker recommended by a friend?
(c) Any broker prepared to purchase them on your behalf?

Question 15

When you have given an order to purchase or sell a certain share:

(a) Do you specify a maximum price for purchase orders or a minimum price for sale orders?
(b) You are happy to purchase or sell at whatever price you get?
(c) You let your broker decided at what price you should buy or sell?

Question 16

What is your primary concern when you purchase a share?

(a) Income.
(b) Capital appreciation.
(c) Investment.
(d) All three.

Question 17

You wish to invest in shares the ₹ 50,000 that you have received on the maturity of your Public Provident Fund account, would you purchase a share:

(a) Recommended by your brokers?
(b) Tipped as a "growth share" by an investment paper?
(c) Suggested by a friend?
(d) Whose name catches your imagination?
(e) Picked at random from the newspaper?

(f) Only after you have studied all the available information on the company and are convinced that the company is managed well and its prospects are good?

Question 18

You have ₹ 10,000 to invest in shares. Would you:

(a) Subscribe to the initial issue of a company being floated?

(b) Subscribe to the rights issue of an existing company?

(c) Purchase shares from the stock market?

Question 19

A company in which you have invested is holding its annual general meeting at a date and time that it is convenient to you. Do you:

(a) Ignore it and not attend?

(b) Attend as a spectator?

(c) Not only attend but actively participate?

Question 20

After purchasing a share, do you keep a check of the movement of the share price?

(a) Daily.

(b) Weekly.

(c) Monthly.

(d) Sometimes.

(e) Never.

Question 21

You subscribed to the shares of Nikhila Ltd. and were awarded 100 shares. The price tripled in 4 months to ₹ 300. Would you:

(a) Sell and book profits?

(b) Hold on and see how it will fare for another six months?

(c) Purchase some more shares in the expectation of the prices rising?

Question 22

A share that you have, has fallen in price by 10 per cent: Do you:

(a) Sell immediately?

(b) Hold onto the share in the expectation of the price recovering as the company is intrinsically good?

(c) Sell the shares if it falls a little further?

Question 23

After buying a share do you ever get sentimental or attached to them to such an extent that you are reluctant to sell them?

(a) No, never.

(b) Yes, often.

(c) One or two.

Answers of Quiz 2

	Your Answer (a/b/c/d)	Your Score
1. a = 1; b = 3; c = 1 d = 0; e = 0	☐	☐
2. a = 1; b = 3; c = 1, d = 4;	☐	☐
3. a = 0; b = 0; c = 2 d = 0; e = 3; f = 4	☐	☐
4. a = 0; b = 1; c =2; d = 3;	☐	☐
5. a = 3; b = 4; c = 2	☐	☐
6. a = 1; b = 2; c = 3; d = 4	☐	☐
7. a = 4; b = 3; c = 2	☐	☐
8. a = 0; b = 1; c = 3	☐	☐
9. a = 0; b =1; c = 3; d = 0	☐	☐
10. a = 0; b = 1; c = 3	☐	☐
11. a = 0; b =1; c = 3	☐	☐
12. a = 1; b = 0; c = 3	☐	☐
13. a = 1; b = 1; c=2; d = 3	☐	☐
14. a = 3; b = 2; c = 1	☐	☐
15. a = 3; b = 1; c = 2	☐	☐
16. a = 2; b = 2; c = 3; d = 3	☐	☐
17. a = 1; b = 2; c = 1; d=0; e = 0; f = 3	☐	☐
18. a = 1; b = 2; c = 3	☐	☐
19. a = 0; b = 1; c = 3	☐	☐
20. a = 4; b = 3; c = 2; d = 1; e = 0	☐	☐
21. a = 1; b = 3; c = 2	☐	☐
22. a = 1; b = 3; c = 2	☐	☐
23. a = 3; b = 1; c = 2	☐	☐
Your Total		

If you scored 25 and below:

You are not really interested in shares and are just purchasing them because everyone else is purchasing them. You would be much better off investing your money in risk free public sector bonds or depositing them in banks.

If you scored between 26 to 55:

You are basically a beginner. You are reasonably cautious which is good. You should make the effort of reading more on companies, trends in industry, etc. This will stand you in good stead.

If you scored between 56 to 70:

You are a steady investor. You are on the right track you are aware of what is happening and do not take undue risks.

If you scored more than 70:

Although you are very knowledgeable there is a real danger in your becoming a speculator. You should curb your instincts a little and take care that you do not get carried away in the excitement of it all.

~

Stock Market Glossary

The glossary detailed below is a compilation of the more common terms used by dealers in the Stock Exchange.

Active Stocks: These are shares which are actively traded in the stock exchange, i.e. those for which the highest number of bargains are recorded. These are reported separately as "A" class shares in the business section of newspapers and magazines.

Agent: A firm when it acts on behalf of its clients as buyer or seller of a security. The agent does not own the security at any time.

All or None Order: An order that must be filled completely or the trade will not take place.

Allotment Letter: This is a letter received by an investor from a company whose shares he has applied for informing him of the number and value of the shares that have been allotted to him.

Annual Report: A publication that includes the financial statements and a report on operations, issued by a company to its shareholders at the company's year end.

Arbitrage: The simultaneous purchase of a share in one stock market and the sale of the same share on another stock market at prices which will yield a profit

Averaging Down: Buying more of a share at a price that is lower than the price paid for the initial investment with the intent to reduce the average cost per share.

Bargain: This is a deal that has been made and can refer to a purchase or a sale.

Basis Point: One hundredth of a percentage point

Bear: A bear is a person who is in the anticipation and belief that the prices will fall sells shares that he does not own (sells forward), expecting to buy the shares at a lower price when he has to deliver the shares.

Bear Market: A market in which share prices are falling.

Beta: A measurement of the relationship between the price of a share and the movement of the whole market.

Blue Chip: This is a term used to describe shares of the best and most respected companies.

Bonus Issue: A bonus issue is the issue of shares of a company to existing shareholders in proportion to the number of shares held by capitalizing reserves.

Bull: A bull believes that prices will rise and therefore buys shares intending to sell them when the price rises.

Bull Market: A market in which share prices are rising.

Business Day: Any day from Monday to Friday excluding statutory holidays

Closing of Books: Periodically a company closes its books. This is to establish a cut off date for the payment of interim dividend, final dividends, bonus shares, rights shares and the like. This can be done more than once a year and the dividends, etc. are given to those whose names are registered as the owners of the shares on the date of the closing of the books. Companies are required to announce in advance the date of closing so that who have purchased shares but not registered them with the company, can do so.

Collateral: Collateral is the security given to secure a loan. Debentures and other loans taken by companies are often collateralized (secured) by stocks or fixed assets of the company.

Commission: Commission is the amount paid to a broker for the purchase or sale of shares and is usually a percentage of the purchase or sale price of the share.

Cum: This means "with." A share purchased "cum div" means with dividend. A share purchased "cum bonus" is with bonus shares and so on. Shares are thus quoted after the announcement of a dividend or bonus, etc. but before the closure of the books.

Delivery: This is the actual handing over of the share certificates and the transfer form duly signed and witnessed.

Dividend: Dividend is the portion of the company's profit that is distributed to the share holders. This is usually declared as a percentage of the face value of the share and is in effect the income the share holder earns on his investment.

Equity Shares: Equity or ordinary shares are the shares that have the right to the profits of a company after preferential shareholders have been paid and between which the assets of the company are distributed after all other claims have been satisfied.

Ex: "Ex" means without and shares are sometimes quoted as "ex bonus" or "ex dividend" or "ex right." This occurs when shares are purchased after the books are closed but before the actual dividend or rights or bonus is paid. Investors purchasing shares at this time purchase them without a right to the dividend or bonus or rights as the case may be.

Fully Paid Shares: Fully paid shares are those shares which have been fully paid for (the face value).

Forward Purchase: A forward purchase is when one agrees to purchase shares at a future period at a certain price. He does this in the belief that the prices will rise.

Growth Stock: The shares of companies that have enjoyed better than average growth over recent years and are expected to continue their limb.

Hedge: A strategy used to limit investment loss by making a transaction that offsets an existing position.

Income Stock: A share with a solid record of dividend payments which offers a dividend yield higher than other equity shares.

Index: A statistical measure of the state of the stock market, based on the performance of shares such as the Sensex and Nifty.

Initial Public Offering (IPO): A company's first issue of shares to the general public.

Inside Information: Non public information pertaining to the business affairs of the company that can affect the company's share price should the information be made public.

Insider Trading: Trades in shares by a person based on material information that is not public knowledge.

Letter of Regret: A letter of regret is a communication received from a company informing one of the company not allotting any share.

Letter of Renunciation: When an offer of a right to subscribe to shares or debentures is made to a shareholder he is offered a right to renounce the shares he is entitled to in favour of another person who then steps into the shoes of the shareholder. This person, however, can only apply up to the number of shares that have been renounced in his favour.

List Closure: This is the date upto which application from the public for an issue of shares / debentures would be accepted.

Listed Stock: Shares listed on the Bombay Stock Exchange or the National Stock Exchange.

Market: The general situation in regard to the rates at which shares are purchased and sold When prices are low it is often stated that the market is depressed. Markets are described as bullish, bearish and the likes to reflect investor sentiment at the period of time.

Market Capitalisation: Total value of the issued shares of a publicly traded company. It is equal to the share price multiplied by the number of shares outstanding.

Market Order: An order to buy or sell a share immediately at the best current price.

Nominal Value: The nominal value is the face value of a share. If the face value of a share is ₹ 10 then it may also be stated that its nominal value is ₹ 10.

One for One: This meant to denote that in a bonus issue declared a bonus share is given for every share held.

Oversubscribed: A company may offer for sale a certain number of shares. If applications are received for shares in excess of the number offered, the issue is termed to be oversubscribed.

Par: Par is another term for the face or nominal value of the share. When an issue of ₹ 10 shares are offered at par it means that the ₹ 10 shares are being offered at ₹ 10 per share.

Pari Passu: This is a latin term and means "having equal rights." When shares (bonus or otherwise) are issued *pari passu* with existing shares it means that the new shares would be equal to and have identical rights with the existing shares.

Partly Paid: Partly paid shares are those whose nominal shares have not been fully paid up. If only ₹ 5 has been paid on a ₹ 10 share, it is termed as partly paid.

Passed Dividend: A company is termed to have "passed dividend" if it has not declared its usual annual dividend.

Penny Stocks: Low speculative issues of stock selling at less than ₹ 1 a share.

Portfolio: Holdings of shares of an individual or institution.

Price Earnings Ratio: A shares last closing market price per share divided by the latest reported 12 month earnings per share.

Private Placement: The private offering of a security to a small group of buyers.

Rally: A brisk rise in the general price level of the market or price of a share.

Record Date: The record date is the date by which a person's name should be registered and entered in the books of a company as the owner of the shares to entitle him to receive the declared dividend.

Scrip: This is another term for a share.

Share Certificates: Share certificates are documents proving a person's ownership of shares.

Short Sale: A short sale occurs when a person believing that the shares will fall, sells shares that he does not own with the intention of purchasing the shares at a lower price at the time delivery has to be made. This is also known as a forward sale.

Split: This occurs when the shares are divided into shares of smaller denomination. ₹ 10 shares may be split into ten ₹ 1 shares. It usually happens when the price becomes unwieldy.

Spot: Spot purchase or sale implies that the deal is for immediate cash and the shares are to be delivered immediately.

Squeeze: A squeeze is a situation by which the prices have moved which forces investors and others to take positions. A fall in prices may squeeze a "bull" to sell in order to maintain or increase his margins.

Stag: A stag is an investor or speculator who subscribes to a new issue with the intention of selling them soon after allotment to realize a quick profit.

Stamp Duty: This is the duty that is payable to transfer shares from one person to another. The purchaser usually pays the stamp duty.

Tip: This is a suggestion to buy or sell a share.

Transfer Deed: A transfer deed is the document that records the transfer of shares and debentures. It should be remembered that the validity of a transfer deed is only up to the date of the book closure of the company.

Trust Deed: The document under which the trust has been created.

Underwrite: Underwriting is effectively a guarantee wherein the underwriter (usually a bank, broker or financial institution) agrees to purchase a certain number of shares in the event the issue is undersubscribed for a certain fee.

Undersubscribed: This term is used to describe an issue when all the shares offered by a company for sale are not subscribed for.

Watered: A company that has issued shares in excess of the real value of business is said to have watered its capital. It is in effect similar to the deficit financing done by some governments.

Yield: Yield is the return earned by investor, or shareholder on his investment.

~